PROGRAMMED TO LEARN

AN ESSAY ON
THE EVOLUTION OF CULTURE

H. RONALD PULLIAM
and
CHRISTOPHER DUNFORD

New York COLUMBIA UNIVERSITY PRESS *1980*

Library of Congress Cataloging in Publication Data
Pulliam, H Ronald.
Programmed to learn.

Includes bibliographical references and index.
1. Learning, Psychology of.   2. Nature and
nurture.   3. Social evolution.   I. Dunford,
Christopher, joint author.   II. Title.
BF318.P84   301.2   79-17941
ISBN 0-231-04838-6

Columbia University Press
New York   Guildford, Surrey

Copyright © 1980 Columbia University Press
Printed in the United States of America

To P.H.K.

and Tink

PREFACE

This book is intended for a wide audience of biologists, psychologists, sociologists and anthropologists, or really for anyone who takes a serious interest in theories about the behavior of learning animals, especially humans. As biologists interested in social behavior, we are distressed by the controversy created by some of our colleagues who have recently explored the adaptive nature of human behavior. They have tried to play a social scientist's game with biologist's rules. Naturally, social scientists have called numerous technical and personal fouls, but before biologists are altogether removed from the game, we hope that everyone will agree that there has been misunderstanding on both sides.

Most biologists spend little time studying human behavior, and perhaps even less time studying the opinions of social scientists who have devoted their lives to the objective study of humans. On the other hand, social scientists have largely ignored the human implications of modern evolutionary theory. In any developing field, the study of human behavior being no exception, the good ideas are bound to be mixed with the not-so-good ones. Every student of human behavior must sort through the muddy waters of the field and decide which ideas to accept and which to reject. It is far too easy to accept or reject entire schools of thought rather than to sort through each point of view for a few good ideas. This problem is the old one of throwing out the baby with the bath water. We believe there are two babies in the bath water of human biology. Since babies need names, we call them social psychology and sociobiology. When these infants are removed from the dirty water that surrounds each, neither can be rejected outright. Each can help the other to mature.

It seems to us that decades of development in intellectual isolation from each other have allowed biological and social scientists to diverge in interests, ideas and especially language to the point where the two types of scientists now find it painfully difficult to communicate. They now live in .two worlds separated by a deep gulf. We feel very strongly that the inhabitants of these two worlds have much to share and can work together toward a modern synthesis which will show that the two worlds are really not so very different when they use the same language.

Much of the recent controversy about human biology has focused on E. O. Wilson's book *Sociobiology*, which is subtitled *The New Synthesis*.[1] Important though it may be, we do not view Wilson's book as a modern synthesis. Rather, it is to us a useful antithesis to the common thesis of some social scientists (particularly behaviorists) that man is free of genetic constraints. A true synthesis would combine the best ideas about human nature from the biological sciences with the best from the social sciences. We cannot claim that our book represents such a synthesis, but it is at least a hybrid of many viewpoints.

In our thinking about learning in animals, we have searched for points of contact which could act as bridges between biological and social-scientific viewpoints. We have written the book to share our bridge-building ambitions, hoping to help in the creation of a common language as the first step toward a common viewpoint. Points of contact are found in a variety of disciplines, in most of which we are inadequately schooled. Though it may not be reflected in our writing style, we are indeed humbled by our limited knowledge of the various subjects we try to present. We are out of our depth much of the time and can only invite the reader to come and dogpaddle with us.

ACKNOWLEDGMENTS

For their comments on drafts of this manuscript, we are grateful to Luigi Cavalli-Sforza, Joe Ingram, George Millikan, Graham Pyke, Vicki Raeburn, Michael Rose, Jack Werren, E. O. Wilson, Bruce Winterhalder, and William Zucker.

We give special thanks to Janice Pulliam, John Maynard Smith, and Tile Barn Cottage.

CONTENTS

Programmed to Learn

CHAPTER ONE

THE GENE'S AGENT

Exploration is not so much a question of covering the ground
as of digging beneath the surface.   —CLAUDE LEVI-STRAUSS[1]

This book is an essay—literally an attempt—to take a fresh
look at the origin and maintenance of cultural diversity. Our
point of view is that to understand the evolution of culture,
we must first understand the evolution of learning.

There are many descriptions of cultural differences between societies and of historical changes within societies,
yet there is no satisfactory framework for explaining or pre-
dicting this diversity and change. Grand theories of cultural
evolution, comparable in scope and purpose to the Darwinian
theory of natural selection, have mostly failed.[2] Perhaps this
failure comes from an inadequate understanding of the
human mind. Indeed, one currently popular view is that
knowledge of the structure of the human mind must be
derived from cross-cultural anthropological studies.[3] We
look at it the other way around and argue that general anthropological principles are most likely to be derived from a
basic understanding of how the human mind works.

The remarkably varied functions of the human mind
almost defy generalization. Nevertheless, we suspect that
this immense complexity is generated by a small number of
principles, or rules of operation. Our approach is to deduce
these principles from a consideration of the biological
evolution of the ability to learn. We start with the evolutionary

problems of simple organisms and build up by steps to an understanding of the human mind as a learning and decision-making device. We hope to show that such a simple understanding can be the basis of a theory of the evolution of human culture.

ᴄᵂᴥ ᴥᵂᴥ

François Jacob once whimsically speculated that the dream of every living cell is to become *two* cells. So wrote Jacques Monod in his natural philosophy of modern biology *Chance and Necessity*.[4] In paraphrasing his colleague, Monod was thinking of the paradox that DNA molecules, with no effort greater than that of binding loosely to compatible nucleic acids, can build cells and organisms that behave as though driven by a purpose—to make as many replicates of the purposeless DNA as possible in the organisms of the next generation. Replication is the end, and the organism is the means.

In his recent book *The Selfish Gene*, Richard Dawkins used the language of purposeful behavior to describe DNA molecules (genes) as replicators building and directing the behavior of organisms (survival machines) to fulfill their "dreams" of replication.[5] The insight and clarity of Dawkins' presentation depends on this beguiling image. The language can lead the unwary imagination to a forest glade where tiny pixies work their will by casting spells on inanimate objects, but such good literary fun should not bother the reader who keeps firmly in mind the true aimless nature of DNA and who remembers that the apparently gene-serving behavior of organisms is an equally aimless consequence of natural selection. Counting on our readers to distinguish the laws of natural selection from the spells of pixies, we will use the image of a purposeful gene to pursue the problem of the origin of learning.

A gene chooses from among alternative courses of action the one that most increases its chances for replication. The problem is that the gene cannot act on its decision directly. It must team up with countless other genes to build a communal survival machine which acts as agent for the genes in pursuing their corporate goal of replication. Each gene passes instructions to the agent by way of its control over some aspect of protein synthesis. Even overlooking the fact that the gene's instruction is only one among thousands and the possibility that the instruction is contradicted or canceled by another gene's instruction, all the genes, individually and corporately, suffer a major handicap. Once delivered to the agent, the instructions are binding and they cannot be effectively changed. This problem especially applies to instructions for the agent's behavior in interaction with its environment. If genes respond at all to a changing situation, they act only through their control of protein synthesis—far too slowly to affect the course of rapid interactions. Since they cannot monitor their agent's performance and amend their instructions accordingly, the genes must issue instructions which somehow anticipate all the events of their agent's lifetime.

The genes are like investors who cannot change or cancel their original instructions to their stockbrokers. A gene investor can choose, from among hundreds of available stocks, the ones that look likely to increase in value. It then instructs its broker to buy so many shares of such-and-such stocks and to sell these shares on a specified date. Between the dates of purchase and sale, the values of the stocks are subject to a multitude of generally unpredictable up and down pressures. No matter if the broker receives information indicating that one of the purchased stocks will quickly "go to hell" or that some other stock not held by the investor shows great promise of "taking off." Bound by the investor's instructions, the broker cannot act on the information. There is no point in passing the information back to the gene investor, because it cannot change its instructions. The investor has complete control over the broker but is unable to take advantage of the broker's information about the developing market situation. The shares are sold on the appointed date, and profits or losses are taken. Most likely losses.

In a complex, unpredictable environment, like the stock market, there can be no set of specific instructions that successfully anticipates all eventualities. The investor's best option is to allow the broker sufficient discretion to act alone on current information. Instead of depending solely on experience in previous generations, as the gene investor must do, the broker can use the current "reading" of the market to select promising stocks. Because no advice is forthcoming from the investor, the broker uses personal discretion in deciding what and when to buy and sell. The investor's instructions emphasize strategy rather than details. Having information and instructions on how much money can be used, whether regular income is more or less important than long-term growth, the investor's tax status, how much risk can be taken, and so on, the broker monitors the day-to-day performance of the investor's portfolio and buys, sells, or "sits tight" in response to market developments that are relevant to the investor's strategy.

Investors are reluctant to give full discretion, because brokers make their money from percentage commissions on the purchase and sale of stock shares, regardless of whether their clients make or lose money in the transactions. Commissions are charged to clients. Even so, the interests of client and broker coincide more or less. If the broker successfully follows the client's strategy instructions, there will be more and larger transactions (meaning more commissions) in the future, the broker hopes. If the broker fails, the investor will withdraw the account. Though their goals are complementary, a broker is always tempted to make more transactions than necessary or prudent for implementing the client's strategy. When the broker has complete discretion, the temptation can become acute. In general, the goals of agent and client usually pull in the same direction, but unless their goals are identical, there are conceivable situations which bring the interests of agent and client into conflict. Having won this insight from analogy, we shelve our investment schemes and again directly consider the relation between client genes and their survival-machine agent.[6]

A reflex arc linking stimulus to response is a good example of a specific instruction for survival-machine behavior. The genes can elaborate by making the response depend on the context—that is, contingent on the presence or absence of other stimuli by means of neural inhibition or facilitation. The instructions can be further elaborated to produce a variety of appropriate responses to a single specific stimulus in a number of contexts. As in the stock market analogy, this method of control works well when *all* possible contexts are anticipated. An unanticipated situation can easily render the survival machine useless. To solve the problem, the genes can specify a set of possible responses and let the survival machine choose the best one, basing its evaluation on information about the current situation. The difficulty is in providing the machine with a useful definition of "best" response.

For the genes a good response enhances the probability of their replication in the next generation of survival machines. How is the machine supposed to calculate these probabilities? It cannot. Given the general instruction to "do whatever contributes to your survival and reproduction" (hence the replication of client genes), the machine would have to try an option long enough to see if it survived and reproduced, by which time it would be too late to try another option. Analogously, it does no good for a runner to decide to speed up when he sees he has lost the race. He must speed up when he falls behind his competitors. Both runner and survival machine need decision criteria which are closely associated with their goals but which give early and frequent indications of how well they are performing en route.

What we are talking about is learning. The survival machine finds itself in a new situation, tries a behavior and has a bad experience. The machine then tries another behavior, and if the second experience is good, the survival machine repeats the second behavior whenever the situation arises again. This is *trial-and-error learning*. The problem for the genes is to define what is good, or rewarding, and what is bad, or punishing. Given these definitions, the survival machine is instructed to seek rewards and avoid punishments. The first priority of the machine is not replication of its client genes or even its own survival and reproduction. Its immediate aim is to maximize rewards and minimize punishments. The genes can only hope the resulting behavior is consistent with their interests.

Trial-and-error learning can be dangerous, as well as wasteful of time and energy. The genes would do better if their survival machine could acquire its information about the current environment in a safer, more efficient way. No alternative presents itself, unless nearby there are some survival machines that have already acquired the necessary information by trial and error. The genes can instruct their machine to observe the experienced machines and imitate their behavior. This solution is less straightforward than it seems. The imitating machine must be given a criterion for recognizing machines more experienced than itself. "Imitate those older than yourself" might do for a general rule. Also, the genes must ensure their machine only imitates others with similar, preferably the same, genetic instructions, so that model and mimic find the same experiences rewarding or punishing. If the machine imitates a genetically related model, their definitions of rewarding and punishing experiences are likely to be similar, if not identical, by descent from a common ancestor. How does the machine know the other machine is genetically related? So go the problems of the genes as they perfect the instructions to their survival machine, much like a computer programmer "debugging" an elaborate program. Each trial run of the genetic program is the life of a survival machine.

ɔﾞﾞﾞ ɔﾞﾞﾞ

Leaving the fairyland image of purposeful genes, we note that as stimulus-response connections are more frequently learned rather than genetically specified, behavioral development of animals is increasingly emancipated from the direct influence of genetic selection. Genetic selection obviously favors animals able to learn from their experiences; but this selection only indirectly affects *what* is learned by its action on the genetically determined definitions of reward and punishment and on the anatomical and physiological limits to what an animal can do. It is also adaptive to learn from the experiences of certain other animals, and development of this social learning further emancipates behavioral development from genetic selection. In the absence of social learning, the lifetime experience of an individual could only influence subsequent generations by changing the probability that the enabling genes would be passed on. Only genes could accumulate experience, and even then only indirectly. The development of social learning started a new way to accumulate experience. A social learner imitates behaviors which are the product of another animal's life experience. The learner modifies and perhaps adds behaviors based on its own experience. A third social learner can then imitate these behaviors and gain the benefit of two lifetimes worth of experience. And so on. This is cultural evolution. *It owes its origin and its rules to genetic evolution, but it has a momentum all its own.*

With the advent of social learning, the evolution of behavior begins to run on two tracks, genetic and cultural, which are interdependent but nevertheless separable.[7] Both genetic and cultural evolution depend on transmission of information from one generation to the next. Genetic transmission is by reproduction. Cutural transmission is by learning from others. The sources of genetic variation are mutation within a population and migration from other populations. Cultural variation comes from innovation within a culture and diffusion from other cultures. Evolution in the former case is the changing of gene frequencies as selection and random drift act on the heritable variation within a population. A genetic trait spreads in the population because it enhances relative fitness; that is, it increases the survival and reproduction of the individuals bearing the trait relative to those without it. Is the same true of a cultural trait?

If animals can only learn from their own parents, an individual must survive to reproductive age and reproduce in order to pass on its cultural traits. Thus, the cultural traits can only spread by reproduction. They increase their representation in the population only by increasing the chances for survival and reproduction of their bearers. On the other hand, when animals learn from nonparents of the older, younger, or same generations, cultural traits can arise and spread to every member of a population without a single birth or death in between.

The evolution of a cultural trait depends on *both* the fitness of individuals who adopt the trait and on the probability that the trait is learned by other individuals. An animal learns to perform a certain behavior because the performance or its result is rewarding. The greater the reward, the more likely the animal will learn the behavior. Immediately comes to mind the image of the genes concocting definitions of rewarding and punishing experiences for use by their survival-machine agents in deciding which responses to repeat and which to avoid. For animals that engage in social learning, imitation of certain other animals may be one of the experiences defined as rewarding. These definitions or decision criteria are the product of genetic selection acting on genetic variation. They are also the driving mechanisms of learning and cultural evolution.

In the next four chapters, we will describe how these driving mechanisms work in individual animals (chapters 2 and 3) and in social groups (chapters 4 and 5). Chapters 6, 7, and 8 explore the importance of these mechanisms to the origin and maintenance of cultural diversity.

CHAPTER TWO

THE CYBERNETIC LIZARD
vs. THE TOXIC ANTS

The learning potential of each species appears to be fully
programmed by the structure of its brain, the sequence of release
of its hormones, and, ultimately, its genes.   —E. O. WILSON[1]

The responses an animal makes to its environment are regulated by neural structures that link sensory input to motor
output. In some animals, the structures do not change with
experience, so the same stimulus always elicits the same response. In other animals, the neural structures do change,
which is to say these animals learn from experience. The
changes in responses are not random; indeed, they may be
species-specific. That is, individuals of the same species
with similar experiences will respond similarly to the same
stimulus while individuals of different species may respond
differently regardless of the similarity of their past experiences. Such differences between species reflect difference in
genetically inherited *learning programs.*[2]

An animal's learning program needs to be adapted to the
contingencies it is likely to face. If a rat is presented a novel
food, it only nibbles a tiny bit even though there may be no
other food available. If the rat becomes ill in the next several
hours, it may never again eat the new food. If the rat does not
become ill, it takes larger and larger portions of the food and
eventually incorporates it into its regular diet. The adaptive-
ness of this behavior, and the learning program behind it, is

attested to by the fact that rats are still major urban pests despite centuries of schemes to poison them.[3]

Even the simplest of learning programs may require fairly elaborate neural structures. To illustrate the design problems of adaptive learning programs, we describe a hypothetical lizard as it searches for food, hypothetical ants. The lizard encounters a variety of visual stimuli which cause distinctive sets of sensory neurons to fire. One such set corresponds to the sight of an ant. When the neural activity representing an ant reaches the lizard's central nervous system, the activity is relayed to a set of motor neurons which activate muscles in a distinctive pattern. The lizard advances on its target. It lunges, mouth opens, tongue flicks, jaws snap. The lizard has eaten an ant. Should it also eat the next ant it encounters?

The lizard's response is controlled at the point of relay between sensory and motor neurons. Neurophysiologists have a very imperfect understanding of what happens in an animal's brain and our knowledge of their understanding is also imperfect, so we do not hope to make more than good guesses about what is happening in the lizard's brain, such as it is. However, we do feel confident in saying that the lizard's brain acts as a cybernetic system, depending on control by feedback from what the lizard has already done. Suppose, for example, the lizard finds both red ants, which are toxic, and black ants, which are not. It could be programmed so that only the set of sensory neurons representing *black* ants is connected to the eating response. Alternatively, the lizard could be programmed to learn which ants to avoid, using feedback from previous experience to control its responses.

Suppose the lizard is initially programmed to eat any ant, regardless of its color. The lizard then needs to evaluate the results of each ant-eating experience. That is, it must also be programmed to classify the neural input from the red-ant toxins as a negative sensation and, perhaps, the input from black-ant juices as a positive sensation. The lizard must also store information about the circumstances and results of each experience in its brain for future reference. That is, it must be programmed to store information like "red ant, eaten, unpleasant." Also the lizard needs to recall the appropriate information when it next encounters an ant. That is, it must be programmed to recognize the new ant as similar to some of the ants already eaten so that it can benefit from its memories of past experiences as it decides whether to eat or move on.

With evaluation, storage, and recall considered as neural processes, there arises a flurry of unanswered questions which we prefer to avoid. However, we must make assertions about some aspects of these three processes in order to develop our train of thought. In the case of evaluation, we assume the existence of a neural mechanism in the lizard's brain which classifies as unpleasant the sensory neuron message about the presence of toxin. We do not imply that lizards necessarily experience pleasant and unpleasant sensations in the same subjective way as do humans. Rather, we simply mean that the brain automatically classifies sensations in such a way as to make the behaviors preceding certain sensations more or less likely to be repeated.[4] The lizard's program then is to eat ants, to classify the taste of toxic ants as unpleasant, and to avoid responses that lead to unpleasant sensations. A genetic program producing the neural architecture that does this is favored by natural selection, because it leads to the development of lizards that avoid poisoning themselves.

The lizard must identify toxic ants by experience when the distinguishing features of toxic ants cannot be anticipated generations in advance. Indeed, in the next canyon over, red ants may be palatable and black ants toxic! Each lizard is programmed to make its own discoveries using the unpleasant taste as a warning signal that stops the lizard before it consumes a lethal dose of toxin. The genetically programmed connection of the toxin-sensing receptors to the neural mechanism classifying the sensations as unpleasant is the genome's only way of indicating that toxin is to be avoided.[5] We call the toxin a *primary reinforcer* because the genetic program specifies that the neural input into the brain from the toxin receptors is to be classified as unpleasant. Reinforcers may be either positive or negative and form the basis on which an animal evaluates its responses.

If the lizard can remember what the unpleasant-tasting ants looked like, it soon discovers that red ants are the ones to be avoided. Of course, the lizard must first be able to distinguish red from black. We have already said that the lizard must be able to store the information "red ant, eaten, unpleasant" and so on. Generalizing, we assert the lizard remembers the stimulus, its own response and its evaluation of the results (subsequent stimuli). We think of an evaluation as a signed value on a positive-to-negative scale. Whether the stimulus-response-evaluation memory trace is stored in the brain as a single unit or as separate components, we assume the components can be recalled as a unit when the lizard sees another ant. Most likely, the recalled information gives some of the same pattern of neural activity as was generated by the original incoming information. Somehow the neural activity created by the sight of a new ant pulls out of storage matching patterns of neural activity corresponding to previously encountered ants along with associated neural activity patterns corresponding to previous responses and evaluations.

Now, suppose a naive lizard has so far found and eaten only two ants, one red and one black. Its third encounter is with a red ant. It recalls the unpleasant experience of eating

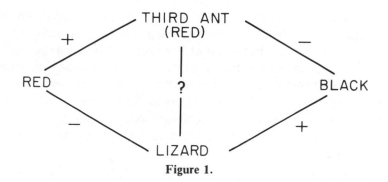

Figure 1.

the first red ant and the pleasant taste of the black one. The only difference the lizard can remember between the two ants is in their color. It might evaluate the third ant by comparing it to the first two, as shown in figure 1. The line from lizard to red ant represents the lizard's evaluation of the ant, which is negative. Similarly, the line from lizard to black ant is positive. The line from red ant to third ant represents the relative stimulus similarity between the two ants. As they are both red, the line is positive. The line between the black ant and the third ant is negative, because they have different colors. The line from lizard to third ant represents an *a priori* evaluation the lizard can make, using the information in the remainder of the graph. We assume the lizard's brain follows a simple consistency rule. The rule says, in effect, if one such object is bad, then any very similar objects are probably bad as well. More precisely, in terms of the linear graph, the two triadic "cycles" in the graph (lizard-red-third and lizard-black-third) must each be positive when the signs of the three component lines of the cycle are algebraically multiplied. No matter, for now, that two types of lines, one for similarity and one for evaluation, are mixed in the calculation. For both cycles, the products are positive only when the question mark becomes a minus. The lizard's *a priori* evaluation of the third ant is negative, so as to be "consistent" with past experience.

We do not even pretend that the lizard's brain makes such algebraic calculations, but whatever happens inside that little head, we assert the lizard's behavior is made consistent with past experience by the operation of some genetically programmed neural structure equivalent in operation to what we have conjectured here. We shall return to the problem of consistency in later chapters.

If the lizard's behavioral responses are to be adaptive, its innate tendency to eat ants must be overcome when the ants are toxic. This genetically programmed tendency is in neural fact a relay of some sort in the brain which facilitates the firing of the "eating" pattern of motor neurons when the "ant" pattern of sensory neurons starts firing. In our example the *a priori* evaluation of the third ant encountered must somehow inhibit this relay. If the inhibition is not strong enough, the lizard goes ahead and eats the third ant and is negatively reinforced. When the next red ant is found, the memories of the two previous unpleasant experiences combine to produce an even lower *a priori* evaluation (i.e., greater inhibition of the relay). Eventually, the accumulated memory of "red ant, eaten, unpleasant" will produce enough inhibition to prevent the eating response. Of course, the lizard continues to eat black ants, because the black color does not inhibit the innate tendency. In fact, if the black ants have a pleasant taste, the accumulated memories of "black ant, eaten, pleasant" will facilitate the eating response.

Our hypothetical lizard has so far lived in a clear-cut, hypothetical world, where red is bad and black is good. The real world is ambiguous. Bad is not so easily told from good. For instance, red may not be easily distinguished from black due to gradations between them, or red may be bad sometimes and good sometimes. Rephrasing the two problems in terms of the linear graph, the similarity and evaluation lines are neither simply positive nor simply negative. They can be graded on a continuous value scale running from very positive (very similar or very good) through zero (neutral) to very negative (very different or very bad) with all possibilities in between.

Imagine that the third ant in the linear graph is dark red, almost black. The lizard might see a weak similarity to both the red ant and the black ant eaten earlier. Evaluations are probably weighted by stimulus similarity. If so, the negative evaluation of the red ant is only weakly applied to the third ant, because the third ant only vaguely resembles the red ant. The weakly negative *a priori* evaluation is further weakened by the third ant's vague resemblance to the black ant, which was positively evaluated. The weak positive may cancel the weak negative, leaving the lizard with a neutral *a priori* evaluation. If the lizard eats the third ant and if the result is pleasant, the memory of the third ant experience might be integrated with the black ant experience or be put in a separate storage-recall category, depending on the complexity of the lizard's stimulus classification.

Consider the existence of an ant that is jet black in front and bright red on the rear. Such ants do exist. To the naive lizard this ant might look very much like both the red ant and the black ant at the same time. This stimulus would then recall memories of both red and black ants creating strongly contradictory *a priori* evaluations of the bicolored ant. Conceivably, the positive and negative evaluations could be equally strong, and counterbalanced in such a way that the lizard is torn between two responses, to eat or to continue its search. It might just stare at the ant, unable to eat it or to ignore it. The resolution of this conflct might depend on some other stimulus or on recall of some other relevant experience.

Then there is the problem that red ants may not always be toxic. The lizard's evaluation after eating ten red ants will be less negative if only eight, rather than all ten, were toxic. The lizard's brain must integrate the results of the ten trials to produce the neural equivalent of a single signed value on a positive-to-negative numerical scale. Likewise, the several experiences with black ants are integrated to give another signed value. If an occasional black ant were toxic, the signed value is lower than if all were palatable. When given a choice of ants to eat, the lizard chooses the color with the most positive (or least negative) value.

Now let us make life even more difficult for our hypothetical lizard by putting it in a world where all ants look identical, but some are toxic and others are not. No matter how many ants it has eaten in the past, the lizard cannot distinguish toxic from nontoxic until it has actually eaten the ant. To survive the lizard must eat nontoxic ants and avoid eating toxic ants. How is this to be done?

Suppose the ants are found in patches rather than spread evenly or randomly around the lizard's habitat. After eating a few ants in a patch, the lizard might be able to decide that the patch was mainly toxic and move on, or mainly nontoxic and settle down for a good meal. If all ants in a single patch are the same, the lizard has to eat only one to make its decision about the patch. Difficulties arise when toxic and nontoxic ants are mixed together. The lizard then needs a program for deciding whether to stay or leave the patch—in other words, for deciding how many toxic ants it will eat before it decides the patch is too toxic. This learning program must integrate the lizard's experience into numerical evaluations that determine its behavior. What the optimal learning program is will depend on both the numbers of toxic and palatable ants and on how they are mixed. Just as an experimental psychologist can determine an animal's reinforcement schedule in the laboratory, the patch structure of ants determines a natural reinforcement schedule for our hypothetical lizard. The lizard's toxic ant problem is solved by having a learning program which is appropriate for its natural reinforcement schedule. We have found that certain simple models of learning developed by mathematical psychologists offer much insight into the nature and solution of this toxic ant problem.[6]

ᥕᢣᡐ ᥕᢣᡐ

The linear-operator model of learning theory rests on the view that learning is a direct change in probability of a response from one trial to another. Specifically, the probability P_{n+1} of eating an ant on trial $n + 1$ is a linear function of the probability P_n of eating an ant on trial n and the reinforcement v_n experienced immediately after trial n. This is represented in the equation

$$P_{n+1} = \alpha P_n + (1 - \alpha)v_n, \tag{2.1}$$

where α is the *learning parameter* and can vary between 0 and 1. If we take the reinforcement values as

$$v_n = \begin{cases} 0 & \text{if ant } n \text{ is toxic} \\ +1 & \text{if ant } n \text{ is palatable,} \end{cases}$$

then when all ants are toxic, the probability of an eating response tends to zero; when all ants are palatable, this probability tends to one. The model is a special case of Bush and Mosteller's two-operator linear model.[7]

The learning parameter α specifies how the lizard's experiences are integrated to determine its response probability. When α is small, the lizard is very likely to eat the next ant if the last one were nontoxic and very likely *not* to eat the next ant if the last one were toxic. In other words, the smaller the parameter the more the lizard is guided by its most recent experience, the last ant eaten, and the less it is influenced by ants previous to the last one. Conversely, the larger α is, the greater the impact of the early experiences and the less the influence of recent experiences on the lizard's eating decisions.[8]

The optimal learning program for the lizard depends on the mixture of toxic and nontoxic ants in the lizard's environment. If the ants live in colonies of like kind, the lizard need eat only one local ant to decide that the remaining ants are likely to be all toxic or all nontoxic. What is the point of trying another ant if it is likely to be toxic, too? In this case where toxic and nontoxic ants occur in discrete patches, a low value of α is adaptive, because it leads to eating the next ant if the first were palatable and avoiding the next if the first were toxic. On the other hand, if toxic and nontoxic ants are more randomly mixed with one another, there is no information in the last ant eaten as to what the next ant will be. In this case a large value of α may be adaptive since it makes the response probability more responsive to the overall proportions of toxic and palatable ants than to the last kind of ant eaten. It is a reasonable assumption that for a given spatial mixture of toxic and palatable ants, natural selection favors the learning program (specified by α) that maximizes the fraction of palatable ants in the lizard's diet.[9]

The model used above is written in terms of probability of eating. We said earlier that the lizard's decision to eat an ant is initially determined by an innate tendency towards ant-eating and is subsequently modified by its evaluations of actual ant-eating experiences. Rather than say the decision is deterministically set by these evaluations, we might say the probability that the lizard will eat the ant is an unspecified function of the lizard's *a priori* evaluation of the ant. To deal with this, equation 2.1 can be modified to

$$V_n = \alpha V_{n-1} + (1 - \alpha)v_n, \qquad (2.2)$$

where V_{n-1} is the *a priori* evaluation of the stimulus-response pair before trial n, v_n is the reinforcement from trial n, and V_n is the new, integrated evaluation *after* trial n. The way v_n is integrated with V_{n-1} to yield V_n is determined by the parameter α. The probability P_{n+1} of eating the next ant encountered is an unspecified function of V_n, the new *a priori* evaluation. The probability and the evaluation are not identical if only because the probability is restricted to values from 0 to 1, whereas the evaluation can be positive or negative and is not necessarily bounded by $+1$ or -1. Equation 2.2 is more general and realistic than equation 2.1, because the reinforcement from a particular trial can be positive or negative in equation 2.2 but only positive in equation 2.1.

Leaving the hypothetical world of our lizard, we use a real bird to illustrate the general point. Peter Klopfer has shown that when an Egyptian vulture first sees an ostrich egg and a stone, it picks up the stone and breaks the egg.[10] What will happen if the egg is empty so the vulture gets no food reward for its effort? Referring to equation 2.2, we can say that if the learning parameter is $\alpha = 1$, the lack of reward has no effect. The vulture will break the next egg and the next and the next whether or not it gets anything to eat as a result. Learning does not affect the initial evaluation V_0, which is the innate tendency set by the genetically designed neural linkage between the sight of egg and stone and the response of picking up and breaking. On the other hand, if α is less than 1, the vulture will eventually learn to give up. If $\alpha = 0$, the vulture would give up after the first try. While the model allows that the innate tendency can determine the behavioral response for life, it also shows that the innate tendency can have a very minor effect on later evaluations as the animal accumulates experience. To show this effect more clearly, we rewrite equation 2.2 as

$$V_n = \alpha^n V_0 + (1 - \alpha) \sum_{x=1}^{n} \alpha^{n-x} v_x, \qquad (2.3)$$

where the first product (before the plus sign) represents the residual innate tendency and the second product represents the accumulated reinforcement experiences. Since α is less than 1, the effect of the innate tendency decreases geometrically and eventually becomes insignificant. As a result, there is no clear-cut difference in this model between a genetically determined response and a learned response.

Our argument is that the genes, by controlling the neural development of the brain, set a learning program that determines how flexible or stereotyped an individual's behavior will be. Initial responses may be genetically programmed, but any innate tendency may be modified by experience with reinforcers, such as toxins or good-tasting juices. A learning program must include both what external stimuli are primary reinforcers and the manner in which experience with these reinforcers is integrated to form and revise evaluations of responses already tried by the animal.

CHAPTER THREE

EMOTION AND DECISION

... there should be a sweetness to life when it accords with the adaptive wisdom of evolution. —DAVID P. BARASH[1]

Like the cybernetic lizard, modern electronic computers can be programmed to make decisions. Computers can identify and evaluate alternatives and choose a course for action. When the goals of artificial and animal decision makers are similar their successful design features are probably also similar, though arrived at by very different processes and with very different materials. A human programmer works toward a conscious goal, making purposeful changes anticipated to improve the program's performance. On the other hand, natural selection can only promote the best of whatever is made available by careless mutation. Purposeless tinkering with genetic messages is hardly a formula for rapid progress,[2] but given enough time, the method works well enough. Over the billion years of life on earth, the natural programming method has produced decision-making organisms far more sophisticated than any machines yet produced by humans. Nonetheless, because the simpler, artificial decision systems are easier to understand, they may give us insights into the design of animal decision-makers, much the way airplanes have helped reveal how birds fly. This is the premise of a remarkable book, *The Biological Origin of Human Values*, by George Edgin Pugh.[3]

Pugh believes that human feelings and emotions are the

decision criteria of the human decision-making system. Pugh's most interesting point is that, in his experience with artificial decision systems, more than one, usually many, decision criteria are needed to make a system function properly. Multiple criteria may be a necessary feature of any successful decision-maker, artificial or animal. To illustrate, Pugh described a computer program developed for HEW to assign children to public schools so as to achieve racial balance in large American school districts. The objective was to eliminate racial segregation with minimum inconvenience and cost. The computer was given information on school, road, and pupil locations and asked to assign children to the various schools. Pugh claimed that to do this efficiently the computer also had to be supplied with a set of values that reflected the desired goals. The original value system used by Pugh's program was simple and "included only the (reward) points for desegregation, together with a very large fixed penalty for any child who had to ride for more than thirty minutes. The resulting assignments . . . showed that complete desegregation, in which all schools had the same percentage of minority students, was possible, even in the largest school districts, without violating the thirty-minute travel limit."[4] However, the resulting system assigned almost all students to distant schools where busing was required. According to Pugh this occurred because "the value structure failed to inform the system that it should avoid unnecessary busing of students."[5] To correct for this, Pugh added a new value, a small point penalty for each student who had to ride the bus. The result was dramatic. The fraction of students bused dropped from over 95 percent to between 10 percent and 30 percent, but the level of desegregation remained just as high. Still no student was bused for more than thirty minutes. The actual computer program used to implement school desegregation had a yet more complex value structure. By adding new values to the system and by adjusting those already built-in, a program was found that made acceptable decisions.

Pugh argued that "experience with artificial decision systems has shown that multiple value components are almost always needed to provide satisfactory adaptive behavior in a complex environment. Systems that are designed to operate solely in terms of a single criterion will almost always behave in ways that seem silly. . . ."[6] Pugh also suggested that the human brain is a multiple-value decision system, and he wrote, "the innate built-in values are experienced as good or bad valuative sensations, such as tactile pleasure or pain, comfort or discomfort, joy or sorrow, and good or bad taste."[7]

In chapter 2, we referred to the toxin in a toxic ant as a primary reinforcer of the lizard's behavior. We argued that the lizard was genetically programmed to regard the toxin as unpleasant. A primary reinforcer is thus a guide to learning, a criterion for decisions. We follow the usual practice of defining a reinforcer as something *external* to the animal. One could justify defining the reinforcer as either the toxic ant, the toxin, the toxin receptor, the sensory neurons, or the part of the central nervous system that classifies the sensation as unpleasant. Without dwelling on the point, we assert that an external reinforcer implies the sensory and neural mechanisms that classify the stimulus. Primary reinforcers imply genetically programmed neural pathways that classify some sensations as pleasant and others as unpleasant. In this sense the primary reinforcers correspond to what Pugh called "innate, built-in values." Specific primary reinforcers arouse sensations that humans call feelings or emotions.

We maintain that the evolution of emotions can only be understood in terms of genetic selection for decision criteria to guide learning. Genes exert control over the behavior of their survival machines by controlling the development of the neural mechanisms that determine which experiences evoke which emotions. Emotions and the reinforcers that evoke them are indicators of comfort and, as such, are bases for evaluating experiences.

⚜ ⚜

Over a century ago, Charles Darwin wrote *The Expression of Emotions in Man and Animals*.[8] Darwin argued that emotions in animals can be detected in the same way as they are detected in humans—by an individual's behavior, in particular, the facial expression. For example, Darwin wrote in his section on primate anger, "A young orang, made jealous by her keeper attending another monkey, slightly uncovered her teeth, and, uttering a peevish noise like *tish-shist*, turned her back on him. Both orangs and chimpanzees, when a little more angered, protrude their lips greatly, and make a harsh barking noise. A young female chimpanzee, in a violent passion, presented a curious resemblance to a child in the same state. She screamed loudly with widely open mouth, the lips being retracted so that the teeth were fully exposed. She threw her arms wildly about, sometimes clasping them over her head. She rolled on the ground, sometimes on her back, sometimes on her belly, and bit everything within reach."[9] Later, in a section on astonishment and terror, Darwin related the following story.

> A living fresh-water turtle was placed at my request in the same compartment in the Zoological Gardens with many monkeys; and they showed unbounded astonishment, as well as some fear. This was displayed by their remaining motionless, staring intently with widely opened eyes, their eyebrows being often moved up and down. Their faces seemed somewhat lengthened. They occasionally raised themselves on their hind-legs to get a

better view. They often retreated a few feet, and then turning their heads over one shoulder, again stared intently. It was curious to observe how much less afraid they were of the turtle than of a living snake which I had formerly placed in their compartment; for in the course of a few minutes some of the monkeys ventured to approach and touch the turtle. On the other hand, some of the larger baboons were greatly terrified, and grinned as if on the point of screaming out.[10]

It is clear from these examples that Darwin assumed that the facial expressions of monkeys and men are homologous and express the same underlying emotions. Darwin's assumption is a claim for homology at two levels—homology of behavior and homology of mental structures. It does not necessarily imply homology of subjectively experienced mental states. That is, even though humans may share homologous emotional structures with other animals, humans may experience conscious sensations not experienced by other animals. For our arguments we assume only the following: 1) specific neural structures involved with emotional reinforcement of behavior are genetically inherited; 2) similar environmental stimuli activate homologous emotional structures in different species; and 3) activation of similar emotional structures has a similar effect on subsequent behavior in different species. Our approach is to treat the emotional structures as "black boxes" and to study emotions by studying the input and output of the black boxes.

A serious problem for an unambiguous discussion of emotion is in enumeration and naming. Just how many emotions are there? We have come to prefer the four categories Darwin used in his discussion of emotions in primates. These are:

1) painful emotions and sensations
2) pleasure, joy, and affection
3) anger
4) astonishment and terror

or more simply, pain, pleasure, anger, and fear. We use these categories more for convenience than because of any conviction that they are the four irreducible elements of emotion. We allow that they might be combined, subdivided, or added to. Still, these four are distinct emotional states about which a great deal is known from scientific observation and experimentation.

✢ ✣

We all have difficulty describing the subjective experience of emotion, even of a straightforward one like pain. As Virginia Woolf put it, "let a sufferer try to describe a pain in his head to a doctor and language at once runs dry."[11] Patrick Wall, director of the Cerebral Functions Group at University College, London, wrote,

> Pain is. My pain as it grows is an imperative obsession. Your pain is a different matter. I observe you and listen to you. I sympathise by guessed analogy. . . . Doctors and patients become extremely angry with each other where there is a mismatch between disease and the amount of pain the doctor expects, especially if the patient fails to respond to accepted therapy. At this point the doctor begins to question if the pain is real or in the mind. What is this curious question asked by the observer but never by the person in pain?[12]

Some people are born without the ability to feel pain, though in all other respects they are normal. Lest you become envious, listen to what Wall has to say about them. "Burns occur because hot things are not noticed. Fractures may not attract attention and go untreated. These people quickly learn to use other cues to avoid dangerous situations but this is not enough. The commonest sign in these patients is severe joint disease originating from the failure to guard a limb after the minor sprains and insults to which we subject ourselves in the most careful of living."[13] People without pain experience extensive burns and bruises as children and frequently chew their own tongues along with their food.

Pain clearly is a guide to learning and produces adaptive behavior. Animals quickly learn to avoid behaviors that increase pain and to repeat those that decrease pain. Since pain generally signals injury of some sort, animals thus learn to avoid injury. However, it is curious how readily pain can be ignored. We are all familiar with stories of Eastern religious men walking on beds of hot coals or of rugby players continuing the game with separated shoulders. In Western society, childbirth is generally considered a painful experience for the mother. Yet in some societies women show no signs of distress during childbirth and may continue working in the fields until minutes before the child is born. In one society, it is the husband who gets into bed and groans with great pain as his wife easily bears the child! The husband then stays in bed to recover from his great ordeal and takes care of the infant while the mother returns to the crops.[14]

Wall points out that in conditions of extreme anxiety such as might be experienced in battle (or rugby), the onset of pain and real awareness of injury may be delayed for hours. Apparently all of the evidence agrees that these pain-free states are associated with massive discharges of nerve impulses from the injured area. The reception of the injury signals is repressed by nerves descending from the brain. The activation of neurons in the reticular formation, which controls attention, can inhibit injury messages to the brain. The analgesic effects of narcotics such as morphine appear to result from these drugs activating these same descending nervous pathways. According to Wall, a naturally "occurring substance in the brain, enkephaline, has narcotic properties and it seems likely that the nervous system normally activates this descending control by releasing its own narcotic."[15]

If pain is an injury message, why should this message ever be repressed? The perception of pain leads to adaptive behavior when it results in behavior which in reducing pain also reduces injury. Moving away from a hot spot usually reduces injury as it reduces pain, but it is possible to jump out of the frying pan and into the fire. If the pain signal increases the chances of jumping into the fire, then repression of pain is called for. But how is natural selection to engineer a design that lets the survival machine know when the fire is lit below the frying pan? A rabbit with a broken leg should run from a fox, as best it can, despite any injury already incurred. It would be interesting to know if the mere sight of a predator leads to reticular formation repression of pain. Perhaps, in general, a strong arousal of one emotion (such as fear) represses another (such as pain), if the two emotions lead to conflicting behavior.

❦ ❦

Pain can be expressed in many forms—the pain of extreme heat, the pain of injury, the pain of a stomach ache, even as mental pain or anguish. Similarly, there are many forms of pleasure. It is still a controversial issue among brain physiologists as to whether or not all pain can be referred to a single pain center and all pleasure to a single pleasure center. James Olds found that electrical stimulation of particular parts of the hypothalmus seemed to be rewarding to rats. He wrote, "Although brain reward behavior sometimes does not persist long after the shocks are cut off, while the reward is available the behavior it motivates is intense. When attempts were made to satiate rats' appetite for brain rewards, the animals worked steadily for periods of 4, 6, 8 or even 24 hours and returned for more after resting. To get their reward they even crossed electrified grids which stopped rats starved for 24 hours from running for food. Even more remarkable is the fact that starving rats, forced to choose between food enough to keep them alive and brain reward, chose the brain reward."[16] More recently physiologists have found that stimulation of many areas in the brain, particularly in the limbic system, leads to "brain reward behaviors."

Many stimuli—sights, sounds, odors, tastes—all of the things that an animal likes or that make it feel good—plug into that part, or those parts, of the brain that give pleasure. Pleasure, like pain, is a generalized sensation that is triggered in many specific ways. Genetically prewired connections between primary reinforcers and a pleasure center should evolve so that animals tend to like what is "good" for them. Does the fact that people sometimes like things that are not good for them mean that pleasure is not an adaptive guide to learning? We have argued that learning programs evolve by natural selection to enhance individual survival and reproduction. Some likes and dislikes are genetically programmed into an animal's nervous physiology; others are acquired by association with primary reinforcers. So there are really two questions at this point. Are the genetically programmed primary reinforcers adaptive guides to early learning? And do the *rules* of association and the formation of secondary reinforcers, at least on the average, enhance individual Darwinian fitness? As we will see, the second question is complicated by the very strong role played by social learning, so we shall restrict our attention to the preferences of species where social learning is minimal, or to infants where the influence of social learning is still quite small.

By far the best data base to explore the question "Do animals like the things that are good for them?" comes from studies of food preference. There are two reasons for this. First, food preferences are very well researched in vertebrates, for obvious reasons. Second, food preferences are not constant. Since the same individual may show different preferences under different circumstances, we may ask if the change in preference corresponds to an underlying change in metabolic needs of the individual. On a very gross level, hunger obviously reflects the energetic requirements of an animal. Hunger leads to eating which reduces both hunger and energy deficit. But animals need more than just energy from their foods—they also need vitamins, minerals and protein, which may or may not be present in a diet that is energetically sufficient. Can hunger reflect these specific requirements?

In a classic study published in 1928, C. M. Davis reported on food selection by newly weaned human infants.[17] The infants grew normally and maintained generally good health on a diet they selected for themselves. The choice of foods included a variety of natural, unprocessed and unpurified foods such as milk, apples, peaches, carrots, peas, potatoes, wheat, liver, fish and beef. More detailed studies of "cafeteria feeding" by rats have shown that they too eat a balanced diet and maintain their weight as well as rats on a standard laboratory diet developed especially for nutritional balance. Of course, the types of food available are critical in such an experiment. When experimental rats fail to select a balanced diet, it can usually be attributed to the absence or indigestibility of some essential food. For example, if casein, which is difficult to digest, is used as the only protein source, rats avoid it and may die of protein deficiency.

A review by Nachman and Cole gives many examples of how an animal's nutritive requirements, even as they change with season, age or reproductive state, are reflected by specific hungers.[18] For example, genital licking by pregnant rats is generally thought to be a response to the specific need to conserve salt. Specific hunger for salt has also been reported for humans. A classic case is that of "a 3½ year-old boy with a severe adrenal deficiency who maintained himself by eating table salt by the handful and died when his salt intake was restricted."[19] In the laboratory, a specific hunger for salt can be induced by reducing salt in the diet or by removing the adrenal gland, which normally promotes sodium reabsorption in the renal tubules. Under either treatment rats show immediate preference for sodium salt solutions over pure water even though they have had no previous experience with salt solutions. If a rat is trained to press a bar for a salt solution reward, the resulting rate of bar pressing is proportional to the salt deficit. Sheep, after several days of salt deprivation, become restless and spend more time exploring and tasting. Salt seems to taste better to them than it did before, since they accept salt-rich foods which were previously rejected.

Unlike salt deprivation, thiamine deprivation does not result in an immediate preference for thiamine. Rather, rats given a thiamine-deficient diet prefer any novel food. If the new food does not contain thiamine, preference for it declines after several days. The preference for a novel food is retained only if it contains thiamine. Similar preference for novel foods is caused by diets deficient in riboflavin, pyridoxine, magnesium and calcium. In the words of Nachman and Cole, animals in a state of need can "learn to develop a preference or an aversion to a particular food as a result of the beneficial or toxic consequences."[20]

Calorie-deprived rats greatly increase their consumption of sugar solutions. Since the sweet taste of foods is generally associated with greater specific caloric values, an increase in preference for sweets by food-deprived rats means that the change in preference matches a change in metabolic need. However, the same immediate preference is shown for both nutritive and nonnutritive sugar solutions because both taste sweet. In at least some experiments, the preferences are later adjusted to reflect the nutritive quality, as well as the taste of the food. At any rate, nonnutritive sugars are extremely rare in natural rodent foods, so that preference for *any* sugar solution is normally adaptive under conditions of low food intake.

⤐ ⤏

Let us turn to another emotion—fear. In his book, *Attachment and Loss*, John Bowlby described a number of studies which trace the development of fear in humans.[21] He listed the situations that arouse fear in infants as "being lost or alone, sudden noises and movements, strange objects or persons, animals, height, rapid approach (and) darkness."[22]

Human infants as young as two months old show fear of a rapidly approaching object. Bowlby described the response of infants to the rapid approach of a foam rubber cube, 20 cm per side. When the object "approaches to within 8 inches of a baby's face, without touching him, the infant pulls his head backwards, puts his hands between his face and the object, and cries loudly. The closer the object comes, the louder the cry."[23] This response is much the same as that of an infant rhesus monkey to an expanding shadow projected on a nearby screen. However, if the shadow initially looms large and is then rapidly decreased in size, no fear is shown. Apparently, a stimulus for fear in monkeys and men is the rapid approach of a large object but not the retreat of the same object.

Clearly the newborn infant has had very little opportunity to learn by experience either to recognize or to cope with harmful situations. In the terms of chapter 2 there has been no previous reinforcement to form evaluations. Thus, to cope with potential emergencies, the infant is born with innate responses (crying, startle, and diffuse movements) which adult observers use to detect the infant's fear. These behaviors are adaptive because they alert adults to the approaching object. Also, the infant's arm movements might deflect the object. The same response might not be appropriate for an adult, so the developing child needs a learning program to evaluate alternative responses to fearful experiences. The positive reinforcement which molds new responses comes from the reduction of fear. An approaching object not only elicits the crying response, it also arouses the internal sensation of fear. If the crying leads to a rapid reduction of fear, the evaluation of crying as a response to fear is increased. This view implies that the infant has innate criteria for the reduction of fear. These criteria might include the comforting feeling from being held and rocked by mother, in which case the reduction of fear would usually correspond to a decrease in danger.

In general, fear appears to be reduced by the reappearance of the familiar. This implies that the infant must have or formulate a concept of the familiar. In the first eight months of human life, infants' fear of strangers is little affected by the presence of the mother.[24] In one study, about three-quarters of the infants aged four to six months responded favorably to the presence of a stranger by smiling, cooing or reaching out, regardless of the mother's whereabouts. By seven to ten months, most infants were wary of anything unfamiliar and responded to a stranger with a cry, a whimper or a frown. Often on the first occasion that an infant showed fear of a stranger, the mother was present and the infant compared the two by looking back and forth. By twelve months of age, half the infants withdrew from a stranger when on their mothers' laps, and all withdrew and showed signs of fear when four feet from mother. When infants were tested with male strangers and female strangers, they showed less fear of females, who were presumably visually more similar to the infants' mothers.

Harry Harlow's extensive studies of rhesus monkeys also show that the presence of the mother alleviates an infant's fear.[25] When separated from its mother, an infant monkey shows little interest in play and appears frightened by any unfamiliar object. When the infant is returned to its mother, it stays in close contact and shows more clinging behavior than it did before separation. Even the presence of a surrogate mother reduces fear. When put in a strange room with its familiar dummy mother, a young rhesus first runs to the dummy and uses it as a base for exploration of the room. Separated from the dummy mother, an infant in an unfamiliar room either curls up on the floor, rocking and crying, or runs around the room clutching itself.

Rhesus infants seem to develop a concept of the familiar more rapidly than do human infants. Up to twenty days of age, rhesus infants show no fear of a strange toy but soon thereafter flee to their mothers if a new toy is put in the room. After six weeks, the infants leave their mothers and cautiously approach new toys. Fear-induced behavior can be recognized in most birds and mammals. A principal difference between species appears to be how rapidly the familiar is differentiated from the unfamiliar. Experiments with very young leghorn chicks indicate that they recognize their surroundings as familiar with only 24 hours of exposure and then show fear responses to new surroundings. The speed of development of the concept of the familiar is no doubt inversely proportional to the complexity of the mental representation of the environment.

As infants mature, the stimuli which arouse fear change.

Two- and three-year-old human children report fear of being alone, falling, darkness, strangers, height, loud sounds and snakes. In longitudinal studies, five-year-olds are less afraid of noise and sudden changes in stimulation but are more likely to be afraid of the dark or of imaginary creatures than they were when they were younger. Some of the fears of children are specific to experiences which have in the past proven painful. Thus, a child fears the doctor because of a previous shot. However, some new fears develop without any *direct* experience. For example, children fear imaginary beasts they have never actually seen but have heard about in frightening stories. Also, a negative evaluation of approaching a snake or entering the woods can be formed before a child has had any specific experience with either snakes or woods. Fear-arousing stimuli are a significant portion of the "large chunk of secondary reinforcers" acquired during socialization, which we discuss at the end of this chapter. In humans, and perhaps some other primates, culturally transmitted evaluations based on fear may alleviate the need for many of the genetically programmed tendencies of other vertebrate species.

Our views on fear can be summarized as follows. Newborn infants are programmed to recognize certain stimuli as fearful. These stimuli are the primary reinforcers that arouse fear. Behaviors that alleviate fear are positively reinforced, and those that increase fear are negatively reinforced. Familiar stimuli alleviate fear and thereby positively reinforce behaviors that lead to fear reduction. Familiar and unfamiliar are defined by each individual's early perceptual experience and, thus, an animal can learn what to fear. New fears develop by association with previously fearful and painful experiences. In humans, and perhaps other species, fears can develop from observing (or hearing of) fearful or painful experiences of others. Once established, fears may persist in a population by cultural transmission from generation to generation.

❧ ☙

Anger is closely associated in both popular and technical literature with its behavioral manifestation, aggression. Despite a tremendous interest in aggression, attested to by the sheer volume of scientific and literary treatments, there is very little agreement on its causes and regulation. Anger often leads to aggression, but aggression invites retaliation. We believe that aggression is regulated by a dynamic opposition of the two emotions, fear and anger. In our view, anger, like fear, is a guide to learning, a criterion for decision making.

Niko Tinbergen's famous experiments with stickleback fish show that very specific postures and color patterns elicit aggression.[26] It is unlikely that male sticklebacks have learned through reinforcement experience to court head-down, silver-bellied conspecifics but to attack head-up, red-bellied ones. Similar studies with birds and mammals show that posture, color and odor may all be important in initiating fights. These specific sign stimuli are what we call primary reinforcers. Some animals respond to them with highly stereotyped, prewired, aggressive behaviors. In others, the primary reinforcers may arouse the emotional sensation of anger, as well as an innate tendency to attack. This tendency may be modified by the reinforcement experienced in aggressive encounters. Part of this reinforcement comes, no doubt, from the pain experienced when an animal is injured. But in many species aggressive encounters rarely, if ever, lead to direct physical combat—still the opponents appear to learn from these experiences. We maintain that much of the reinforcement experienced in aggressive encounters comes from the reduction of fear or anger and that it is largely this reinforcement which regulates animal conflicts.

In a territorial conflict, the initial evaluations of attacking and fleeing presumably reflect the past experiences of the two opponents. Individuals who in past encounters have experienced little pain and whose aggressions have been positively reinforced by the reduction of fear and anger on the retreat of an opponent, will have high evaluations of attack. Individuals who have been injured or generally have lost aggressive encounters will have lower evaluations of attack and higher evaluations of fleeing. Thus, the evaluations will reflect, on the average, the fighting abilities of the opponents and thereby the potential costs to them. If size of the opponent or perhaps color patches indicative of maturity increase fear, then the increase in fear will decrease the evaluation of attack, and this too will reflect differences in potential cost. A resident individual will have more to gain by attack than an intruder, and this too may be reflected in the evaluations. More fear is aroused in the intruder who is unfamiliar with the territory—this leads to a devaluation of attack by the intruder. Anger is aroused in a resident individual by the sight of an unfamiliar intruder on the resident's familiar territory, and this anger may be reduced by fighting or by the flight of the intruder. If, by fleeing, the intruder returns to a familiar area, this will positively reinforce fleeing because it leads to a decrease in fear. In this example, the evaluations will approximately reflect the costs and benefits of aggression. How close the approximation is will depend on details of the learning program.

Some evidence indicates that the opportunity to fight itself alleviates anger. Behaviors can be operantly conditioned when the only reward is the opportunity to attack or display aggressively. Monkeys learn to pull a chain to produce an inanimate object which they then attack. Siamese fighting fish learn to swim through a ring and down a runway when the only reward for these behaviors is the chance to perform aggressive displays and fighting movements. Mice will run a runway or cross an electric grid for the chance to fight a submissive mouse.[27] In all of these examples something associated with the attack itself appears to reinforce the behavior. Surely, there are many things which arouse anger in a caged animal and few behaviors which reduce anger. By postulating anger as an intervening variable, we can say that it is the reduction of anger that reinforces these attack behaviors.

In a recent review of aggression in vertebrates, John Archer argued that many situations evoking either aggression or fear behavior are characterized by a discrepancy between experienced and expected stimulation.[28] Anger is aroused when actual reward is less than expected reward. Many vertebrates, including pigeons, rats and squirrel monkeys, are more likely to attack a conspecific when they are only infrequently rewarded for a task than when they are rewarded every time. When rats trained on a continuous reinforcement schedule are suddenly shifted to partial reinforcement, they are likely to attack a conspecific after a nonrewarded trial but not after a rewarded trial. When a rat is thwarted by a physical barrier which prevents completion of a previously rewarded response, it is likely to attack a nearby conspecific. On the other hand, animals are also likely to become aggressive when they receive unexpected punishment. For instance, pain-induced fighting has been reported in ground squirrels, gerbils, hamsters, cats, monkeys, snakes, turtles and chickens. Rats given an electric shock often adopt the same fighting posture as is adopted in socially induced fighting.

All these examples of what elicits attack can be interpreted as representing a discrepancy between the attacker's actual and expected stimulation. Archer argued that an animal maintains "a continuous complex representation of expectancies" based on past experience and that these expectancies are continuously compared to the animal's perception of ongoing events. We do not expect snakes or even gerbils to realize that a conspecific is responsible for a sudden reduction of reward. What we do expect is that animals that are genetically programmed to attack when reward is reduced will, on the average, leave more offspring than those that never attack.

⚜ ⚜

This discussion of pain, pleasure, fear and anger is meant to give the reader a feeling for the concept of emotions as decision criteria. The underlying idea is really quite simple. Remember that the genes had to define good and bad for their agent. The solution has been to create emotional sensations within the animal agent which make it want to avoid "bad" experiences and repeat "good" ones. An animal's evaluation of an experience as good or bad depends on the presence of certain stimuli, the primary reinforcers, which were genetically programmed to trigger either pleasant or unpleasant sensations. As these emotional sensations are criteria for evaluating experiences on which an animal bases its behavioral decisions, it seems appropriate to follow George Pugh's lead in thinking of emotions as decision criteria. We all know from personal experience the turmoil of conflicting emotions. This dynamic tension of counterbalancing criteria provides fine-tuning for behavioral decisions of emotional animals.

A set of emotions genetically linked to a multitude of primary reinforcers is still only a basic tool for evaluating experience. Primary reinforcing stimuli become associated in the animal's brain with other stimuli that occur at the same time and place. An associated stimulus comes to trigger an emotional sensation solely because of its association with a primary reinforcer which triggers that sensation. We call an associated stimulus a *secondary reinforcer*. It is learned rather than genetically programmed. The linear graph example from chapter 2 (figure 1) can be applied to learning by association to show the operation of a simple consistency principle (figure 2). The association between the primary reinforcing stimulus and a second stimulus is shown as a positive line, as is the neural connection by which the primary reinforcer increases the fear emotion. Following the consistency principle used before, the third line must also be positive (fear-increasing) to give a positive algebraic product for the triadic "cycle." We can also assume that the fear-increasing quality of the secondary reinforcer becomes stronger as the association with the primary reinforcer increases. Some sort of fear-increasing neural connection is forged by association.

The possibility of stimulus association with a primary reinforcer allows for stimulus association with a secondary reinforcer, so that chains of associations can build from a single primary reinforcer which anchors the associated reinforcers to an emotion. The consistency principle assures that the as-

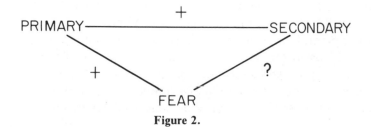

Figure 2.

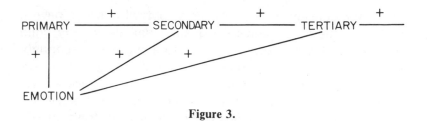

Figure 3.

sociated reinforcers have the same sort of neural connection to the emotion as the primary reinforcer, though the effect may be weakened by tenuous association. Figure 3 shows a chain of associations.

Elaboration of these chains is limited only by the associative ability of an animal's brain. Considering the remarkable development of associative areas in the human brain, it is not surprising that even abstract ideas and structures can have emotional impact on humans far removed from the world of stimuli in which their primary reinforcers and emotions evolved. Human behavior may change rapidly through the generations as secondary reinforcers change, but we see no reason to believe that the anchors for human behavior, primary reinforcers and emotions, have changed in the relatively short time since all humans were hunters and gatherers.[29]

The process of building up an interlocking set of secondary reinforcers from the primary reinforcers need not be repeated completely by each individual. In highly social species, most notably the human, a large chunk of secondary reinforcers may be acquired as a set in the process of socialization. Emotions are still the guides to this social learning, and even though they may be quickly obscured by accumulation of acquired reinforcers, the primary reinforcers still function as anchors to the emotions. Secondary reinforcers may vary between human cultures, but all cultures have a certain similarity or universal quality that allows any child born into one but raised in another to acquire the secondary reinforcers of the adopting culture like a native. We believe this cross-fostering of children is possible because all humans are anchored to the same emotions by the same primary reinforcers, which are universal genetic traits of our species.

CHAPTER FOUR

SHORTCUTS TO LEARNING

The obvious problem with trial-and-error learning is error. Rats only nibble at a new food and if it makes them ill, they refuse to eat any more of it. Too bad if one nibble proves lethal. Medieval kings had a more efficient scheme—they employed food tasters. If the food did not poison the taster, most likely it would not poison the king. Most people would not employ a food taster but might ask a waiter, "What do you recommend?" The principle is similar. We rely on the experience of another individual to shortcut trial-and-error learning. In relying on another individual, we assume a basic similarity in likes and dislikes.

This chapter is about two kinds of shortcuts to learning—imprinting and observational learning. In the case of observational learning the shortcut is obvious. One person learns from someone else's trial and error. But how is imprinting a shortcut to learning?

Animals imprint on mates, foods, and habitats. The parasitic European cuckoo is thought to imprint on its host's nest. Konrad Lorenz popularized the concept of imprinting with his studies of the tendency of young geese and ducks to follow certain moving objects.[1] Lorenz emphasized two characteristics of imprinting. First, imprinting takes place during a restricted period early in the individual's life—the sensitive period. Second, imprinting is persistent; that is, what is learned is not easily forgotten. Imprinting is a specialized and very effective form of learning that occurs during a period of life when parents exert a strong influence on what their offspring learn. It is a shortcut to learning in that the parents, by the control they exert over their offspring's experience, reduce the chances of error involved in learning.

Consider habitat imprinting. It is easy to imagine two very different ways that a bird might learn where to breed. First, the bird might use the trial-and-error plan: pick a habitat, find a mate, build a nest, lay and incubate the eggs, feed the nestlings and hope to fledge young birds. If it works, try the same habitat again. If not, try another habitat. It sounds exhausting and not at all efficient. If a good habitat this year is likely to be a good habitat next year, there is an obvious advantage to a second plan, habitat imprinting. Since the criterion for a good habitat is successful breeding, the very fact of having been born in the swamp means that the swamp is a good habitat, or at least that it recently has been. Habitat imprinting allows the experience of the parents to be transmitted to their offspring by shortcutting trial-and-error learning.

Still there is a serious problem with habitat imprinting. Imagine you are a swamp sparrow. Having been born in the swamp, you prefer to breed in the swamp. But what if one year the swamp goes dry or is overcrowded, so you breed in the adjacent pine forest? The next year there is plenty of room in the swamp again and you return there to breed, but your pine-bred offspring remain in the pine forest, where the breeding is less successful. The problem is that your genotype, which imprints on its early habitat, may be at a disadvantage compared to a genotype which prefers swamp breeding regardless of early experience. That is, your genotype may lose out if the swamp (when available) is always the best place for swamp sparrows to breed, because some of your offspring will breed in the pine forest. On the other hand, if the swamp is the best place to breed for several generations running, and then the pine forest is best for several generations, the imprinting genotype may have an advantage. The relative advantage of habitat imprinting depends critically on the between-generation covariance of habitat quality.[2]

This is an appropriate place to digress briefly and discuss the relationship of imprinting to primary reinforcers and innate response tendencies. Ethologists often discuss the evolution of behavior in terms of *releasers* and *fixed action patterns*.[3] A fixed action pattern is considered to be a complex, instinctive behavior which is "released" in the presence of a specific external cue, or releaser. Lorenz originally defined imprinting as the "process of the acquisition of the object of instinctive behavior patterns."[4] Thus, imprinting can be viewed as the acquisition of the releaser of a fixed action pattern. What might this mean in terms of neural structures and neural development?

Information about an animal's external environment reaches the brain via the activity of specific sensory neurons, which activate specific neurons in the central nervous system. We assume that an external object is represented in the brain as a specific pattern of central neural activity. Long after the object is no longer present in the animal's sensory environment, certain distinguishing features of the object may be stored in the animal's long-term memory as a *stimulus representation* of the original object. We assume that this stimulus representation is a physical structure, either neural or biochemical, which can reactivate part of the same pattern of neural activity that originally represented the external object. We also assume that when the same object is encountered again, it is recognized by a comparison of the central neural activity generated by the object itself and that generated by the stimulus representation in the memory.[5]

Every tiny muscle contraction that plays a role in behavior is activated by specific motor neurons. Their temporal activity pattern is determined by the activity pattern of specific neurons in the central nervous system. As in the case of a stimulus representation, this pattern of central neural activity may be stored in memory as a *response representation*. That is, the animal remembers certain features of its past behavior patterns.

We see an evolutionary progression and a mechanistic continuum from stimulus and response representations that are genetically programmed to those that are formed entirely as a result of individual experience. Imprinting seems to represent an intermediate evolutionary step wherein the stimulus representation (or releaser) is determined by experience but the response representation (or fixed action pattern) is genetically programmed. Consider the case of imprinting of the "following response" by ducklings. The response representation in this case is simply walking, but for walking to become following, a specific object must elicit and orient walking. This object is usually the mother. Though details of the response representation that generates the neural coordination of walking may be modified by experience, we assume that, in broad outline, the response representation is genetically programmed into the physical structure of the central nervous system. This response representation is connected to the area of the brain where the stimulus representation will form. The strength of this neural link is in effect an innate evaluation of following. Because this evaluation is positive, once the duckling imprints (i.e., forms the stimulus representation), the imprinted object automatically elicits following.

P. P. G. Bateson and his colleagues at Cambridge University have studied imprinting of the following response at a molecular level.[6] On the first day after the chicks hatched, Bateson exposed domestic chicks to an imprinting stimulus for varying lengths of time. He found that the longer a chick was exposed to the stimulus, the stronger its preference for the imprinted object over a standard unfamiliar object. On the second day after hatching, one day after training, the chicks were injected with radioactive uracil and later exposed once more to the imprinting object. Two and one half hours after the second exposure, the chicks were killed and their brains were examined for uracil incorporation. The longer the chicks had been exposed on the first day, the lower the rate of uracil incorporation into macromolecules (presumedly RNA) in the anterior roof of the forebrain on the second day. The results suggest that imprinting was correlated with neural differentiation in a specific part of the brain and that the further the development proceeded on the first day, the less the differentiation that needed to occur on the second day when birds were retrained. This neural differentiation may represent the formation of what we are calling the stimulus representation.

꿍꿍 꿍꿍

It should be emphasized that we are talking about a behavioral continuum from situations where both stimulus and response representations are fully defined by genetic development and are unalterable by experience, to situations where either or both representations are partially or fully formed as a result of experience. Imprinting represents one intermediate step wherein the response representation is genetically programmed in some detail but the stimulus representation is largely acquired by experience. What about the other side of the coin? Can the stimulus representation be genetically programmed and the response representation learned? This would imply that an animal innately recognizes a particular stimulus but, in a sense, does not know what to do about it. This hardly makes good adaptive sense unless the stimulus is innately evaluated, in which case we call it a primary reinforcer. The animal is genetically programmed to respond emotionally to a particular stimulus but its behavioral response is not specified. The primary reinforcer acts as a guide to learning.

One way in which a primary reinforcer may contribute to the formation of a response representation is well illustrated by song development in some birds. We prefer to define imprinting in the narrow sense, as did Lorenz, as the process of the acquisition of a stimulus representation to go with a genetically programmed response representation. This definition excludes song development, which some authors have referred to as song imprinting. In song development, it is the response, singing, and not the stimulus, which is acquired, in part, by experience.

Peter Marler and his associates at Rockefeller University have studied in great detail how sparrows acquire their songs.[7] In white-crowned sparrows, only males sing, and each male normally acquires a particular song dialect during its first 100 days after hatching. If deafened before the acquisition period, a white-crowned sparrow develops a totally abnormal song. An undeafened bird reared in isolation learns a song with many normal characteristics. However, only when a young male hears the songs of other males does it develop a characteristic dialect. Marler's experiments support the view that the birds have a genetically programmed neural template of "the basic white-crowned sparrow song." This template is, in effect, an outline for the neural representation and, as such, is embellished by the addition of song phrases of other white-crowned sparrows. Since the specific phrases added to the basic song normally are learned from nearby adults, local song dialects develop and are transmitted culturally from generation to generation.[8]

In our view, the species-specific song of an auditorily intact, male white-crowned sparrow is a positive primary reinforcer. Only when the sparrow compares its own vocalizations to the preexisting template does it learn the basic song. Our idea is that sounds that produce neural activity matching patterns in the template reinforce the singing behavior that produced the sounds. That is, an inexperienced sparrow produces a variety of sounds but is most likely to repeat those that match its neural template of the basic white-crowned sparrow song. When a young bird hears an adult sing, it hears the sound of the basic template mixed with sounds characteristic of the local dialect. These temporally associated sounds then become secondary reinforcers and are incorporated into the song.[9]

The evolution of the vertebrates appears to be characterized by progressively less genetic determination of behavior. What, if any, are the evolutionary advantages to flexible stimulus and response representations that are more and more molded by individual experience? In the case of imprinting of the following response, the chicks and ducklings are not only learning whom to follow but are also establishing mate preferences for later life. Recent studies by Bateson indicate that the preference is not for a mate that looks *exactly* like the imprinted object but instead for a mate that is *slightly* different.[10] Thus, imprinting might lead to the avoidance of inbreeding since an adult chicken will prefer to mate with other chickens but not with mother and perhaps not with siblings who probably look more like mother than do randomly chosen individuals. Similarly, a female white-crowned sparrow may prefer to mate with a male that sounds similar to, but not exactly like, her father. If her brothers sound exactly like her father, then a female would also avoid mating with her brothers. This leads to the intriguing possibility that novel song phrases used by the father might *positively* reinforce a son's singing them but negatively reinforce a daughter's preference for a mate that sings them. By the way, the deleterious effects of inbreeding on reproductive success are as well documented for some bird species as they are for humans.[11]

Food preference may be established by imprinting or by direct observational learning.[12] For example, a rat pup learns to eat the same foods as are eaten by adult members of its colony and to avoid foods avoided by the adults. Apparently gustatory cues in the mother's milk are sufficient for a pup to recognize the mother's diet later. The pup imprints on these cues, and later prefers to eat similar-tasting foods. Also, when a pup eats its first solid meal, it tends to feed in the immediate vicinity of a foraging adult and thus to find similar foods. Food preferences thus established by social learning can lead to striking differences in the diets of different rat colonies even though roughly the same foods are available. For example, rats in some seashore colonies eat mussels while rats in nearby colonies avoid mussels. Individuals from different mussel-eating colonies may even have markedly different techniques for opening mussel shells. These techniques are presumably learned by observation within a colony and thus transmitted socially from generation to generation.

Rats learn a great variety of behaviors by observing other rats. In typical experiments to study observational learning, an untrained rat is allowed to watch the behavior of a trained one. For example, one group of rats may be trained to run a shuttle in order to avoid an electric shock when a buzzer is sounded. Naive rats allowed to watch these trained rats later show a fully conditioned response to the buzzer even when tested alone, though they have never been shocked themselves. Other experiments have shown that rats show fearful behaviors just in response to the fearful behavior of other rats. Many psychologists contend that not only overt behavior but emotional state as well is transmitted between individuals by observation; that is, fear may be contagious. According to this view observational learning is simply a special form of classical conditioning. The model rat is the unconditioned stimulus and imitation is the unconditioned response. The buzzer becomes the conditioned stimulus to the observer rat by its association with the model rat. The reinforcement comes from an empathetically shared emotional state.

Some of the best experimental work on observational learning has been done with cats.[13] In early experiments, observer cats watched model cats learn to jump a hurdle in response to a buzzer in order to avoid a shock. The observer cats all learned the task significantly faster than did controls and some even showed error-free learning. Later experiments with cats showed that kittens learned much more quickly from observing their own mothers than from observing strangers. Kittens who watched their trained mothers push a lever for a food reward learned to push the lever themselves in an average of 3.5 days as compared to an average of 18.0 days for kittens who watched strangers! Significantly, a group of controls that had no model adults never learned the task.

Primates are particularly good at observational learning. For instance, infant baboons may learn food preferences by watching adults.[14] In one experiment, an adult female baboon was taught to discriminate between red banana slices which were palatable and blue ones which were bitter (quinine added). Five infant baboons were allowed to watch the previously trained adult choose banana slices and were then allowed to make their own choices. The infants tasted all of the red banana slices offered them and refused all of the blue ones. Fifteen days later, the infant baboons still preferred red banana slices although they had never experienced the bitter taste of the blue banana slices. This and similar experiments demonstrate that primates pay close attention to what conspecifics do and often shortcut trial-and-error learning by imitating others.

In the experiment described above, the infant baboons were behaving adaptively by imitating the behavior of the adult baboon, since imitation led to the avoidance of a distasteful, possibly poisonous, food. Should an infant always ape the behavior of others? Clearly not if the other is behaving in a way that is *not* good for the infant. Ideally an infant would only imitate the behavior of those individuals who behaved in a way that was good for the infant. Perhaps the infant could be programmed to imitate only the behavior of individuals of a particular sex, age, or dominance, or perhaps only to imitate close kin. Alternatively, infants could be programmed to learn which individuals to imitate. If initially an infant had a weak innate tendency to imitate all familiar conspecifics, it could learn by trial and error which individuals to continue to imitate. Since reinforcers are the infant's guide to learning, the infant would continue to imitate the behavior of those individuals the imitation of whom led to positive reinforcement. Even assuming that all individuals are born with identical primary reinforcers, different experiences would lead to different likes and dislikes so that individuals would soon not share all the same secondary reinforcers. The more one individual imitates the behavior of another, the more similar their reinforcement histories become, so that their secondary reinforcers converge. Conversely, the less one individual imitates another, the more their secondary reinforcers diverge and the less likely one is to find imitating the other rewarding. This feedback can lead to the formation of cliques of individuals with similar likes and dislikes.

In a society with prolonged child care, we expect infants to be most likely to imitate their parents. Juveniles should be very likely to imitate their juvenile playmates, particularly their own siblings since their reinforcement histories are most similar because they imitate the same parents. When juveniles imitate the behavior of adults, they could be more likely to be rewarded by imitating the behavior of dominant adults who have priority of access to scarce resources, than by imitating subordinate adults. Aging leads to increased divergence of reinforcement histories so that adults should be least likely to imitate. If indeed animals learn whom to imitate by trial-and-error imitation, all of these general trends could be reversed by the accidents of a stochastic reinforcement schedule *or* by experimental manipulation.

❧ ☙

Japanese scientists have studied the structure of who learns from whom by observing the diffusion of innovations in several troops of Japanese macaques since the early 1950s.[15] Troops of these monkeys differ in remarkable ways which are almost certainly due to cultural, not genetic, evolution of behavior. For example, members of some troops like to eat eggs while those in other troops do not. These differences extend well beyond simple differences in diet. Paternal care of infants in the birth season is common in the Mount

Takasaki troop but is seldom seen elsewhere. In most troops dominant males prevent young males from mounting females outside the breeding season, but in one troop dominant males commonly allow such out-of-season mounting.

In most troops, macaques do not seem to like sweet potatoes. However in the Koshima Island troop, the monkeys not only eat sweet potatoes, they also wash them first. In 1953, an eighteen-month-old female named Imo innovated sweet potato washing. First her mother, then her playmates and siblings learned to wash sweet potatoes from watching Imo. By 1962, all members of the troop, except infants (who were too young) and adults over twelve years old, were washing sweet potatoes. Prior to the innovation of washing sweet potatoes, all of the monkeys avoided the sea around the island. But to wash the potatoes, they learned to carry them in their hands and wade upright into the water. Soon dabbling and swimming spread among the monkeys.

Later, Imo invented "placer mining" of wheat. Wheat was thrown onto the beach by the scientists as a dietary supplement. Naturally it was difficult to separate wheat from sand. Imo learned to throw handfuls of sand with wheat into the water. Wheat floats, sand sinks. By 1962, most of Imo's agemates were placer mining wheat, but only a few of the older monkeys had acquired the new behavior. Another innovation which spread in the Koshima troop was the "give-me-some" hand gesture. The gesture, made by holding a hand out with the palm up to a human, was first noted in 1960 and rapidly spread to other troop members.

The primatologists at the Japan Monkey Center have now studied the diffusion of similar innovations experimentally.[16] By offering new foodstuffs (wheat, apples, oranges, caramels, etc.) to the Koshima Island and other troops, they have demonstrated some of the complexity of the acquisition process. They have found marked differences between troops in their attitudes towards new foods; some troops readily accept innovations but others reject all innovations. Within a troop, diffusion follows certain predictable paths which depend on the effects of age, sex, dominance and kinship. Young juveniles are most likely to make innovations. These spread rapidly to other juveniles, particularly to play-mates and siblings. Mothers are likely to learn from their own offspring, and innovations may spread from adult females to their mates or to other adults who groom each other. Dominant adult males are the least likely to make innovations or to adopt the innovations of others.

We have argued that learning by observation is less risky than learning by trial and error. We have also suggested that in species with prolonged parental care, infants have a genetically programmed tendency to imitate familiar con-specifics. Individuals learn through experience that imitating some individuals is more rewarding than imitating others. Because secondary reinforcers diverge between individuals with very different experiences, individuals learn to imitate others who have had similar experiences, and these others are often kin.

✿ ✿

Observational learning is the basic mechanism by which information is culturally transmitted from generation to generation. In making this generalization, we do not want to minimize the important role of trial-and-error learning in cultural transmission. We find it useful to think of observation as a source of potential behavior, available for personal experimentation. The observer's initial evaluation of a particular behavior may be positive because of its association with a positively evaluated model individual. Still, only when the experiment is successful in terms of reinforcement is the behavior likely to be added permanently to the observer's own behavioral repertoire.

Behaviors which lead to negative reinforcement are not likely to be repeated and so become unlikely to be observed by others. When circumstances change and a once positively reinforced behavior becomes negatively reinforced, the behavior is likely to disappear from the population. Similarly, when the opportunity or necessity to perform no longer exists, a behavior will drop out of the behavioral repertoire of the population, because younger generations will not see the behavior performed by older generations. The lost behavior can only reappear through reinvention or contact with outsiders who continue to perform it.

There is a twist to the transmission and elimination of learned behaviors. At the point where intergenerational transmission is first broken, members of the older generation no longer perform the behavior even though they once did observe it and perhaps once tried it themselves. Thus, it is very likely that the older individuals retain a memory of the behavior though it is lost from their performing repertoire. A distinction between the repertoires of memory and of performance has no relevance to cultural transmission in any species except our own. Human language allows for linguistic labeling of elements in the mind. Once labeled, these elements can be manipulated in thought and in speech. Thus, speech becomes the only performance necessary to transmit an idea.

We shall return to this distinctly human feature of cultural transmission in chapter 7. First, we want to take a closer look, in chapter 5, at how the human mind works, and then develop, in chapter 6, a method for thinking about cultural phenomena when dealing with entire populations.

CHAPTER FIVE

SOCIAL EXCHANGE AND COGNITIVE BALANCE

The human is such a social animal that it is nearly impossible to separate the effects of social influence from those of personal experience. Human social structure and culture are the result of all participating individuals making individual decisions, but at the same time the social structure and culture weigh so heavily on those decisions that it often seems that the decisions are made for the hapless individual. This chapter is about the social psychology of behavioral choice, and it depends upon a brief review of two social psychological viewpoints—social exchange and cognitive balance. Like most scientists, the social psychologists are drawn into grumpy battlelines, eyeing each other suspiciously, feeling that outright shooting is not really sporting, but nevertheless adamantly refusing to break ranks. Like most outside observers, we fail to see why their differences are not more easily reconciled. Rather than try to sharply define and contrast the viewpoints, we will only draw insights from both to extend our thesis into the realm of human behavior.

Our argument all along has been based on the simple and widely accepted assumption that animals learn to perform behavior that increases reward or reduces punishment and to avoid behavior that causes the reverse to happen. George Caspar Homans started from this same assumption to develop a view of social behavior as exchange of actions which reward or punish the actors involved.[1] We cannot help feeling that Homans would be sympathetic to the way our argument has developed so far. He obviously had to work through the same problems of defining rewards and punishments. The things that humans find rewarding or punishing we have called reinforcers, while Homans called them values (as did George Pugh). Certain emotional reactions to the outcome of the exchange of actions, such as anger and pleasure, Homans called sentiments.

It is worth quoting Homans on the subject of values.

> What makes values infinitely varied is that, besides being born in men and animals, they can also be learned. A value is learned by being linked with an action that is successful in obtaining a more primordial value. Suppose a mother often hugs her child—and getting hugged is probably an innate value—in circumstances in which the child has behaved differently from other children and, as the mother says, "better." Then "behaving better" than others is a means to a rewarding end and is apt to become, as we say, "rewarding in itself." In other words, it is an acquired value. The reward may generalize, and the child may be well on the way to setting a high value on status of all kinds. By such processes of linking, men may learn and maintain long chains of behavior leading to some ultimate reward.[2]

The quote from Homans reminds us of another much earlier one from Darwin. "The movement of expressions in the face and body, whatever their origin may have been, are in themselves of much importance for our welfare. They serve as the first means of communication between the mother and her infant; she smiles approval, and thus encourages her child on the right path, or frowns disapproval."[3]

Social approval as a generalized value (for instance, the mother's hug or a smile) is particularly important to Homans' view of social exchange. Quite often the exchange of rewards or punishments is only an exchange of approving or disapproving acts. Social approval (and more recently, money) can serve as reward for a wide variety of actions, hence the term generalized value. Generalized rewards can be exchanged for any of a wide range of more specific ones.

Exchange theory was actually developed independently by Homans and by Jack W. Thibaut and Harold H. Kelley.[4] It goes beyond traditional economic decision theory to include both immaterial (social and emotional) and material rewards and costs in social relations. Choice is based on the relative profits of alternative courses of action. Thibaut and Kelley introduced the concepts of comparison level (the expected profit of chosen behavior), comparison level of alternatives (expected profit of alternative choices), and outcome (the actual profit from the chosen behavior). When a person's outcome from a chosen behavior is greater than expected, then the person should be satisfied. If his outcome is less than expected but greater than the expected outcome from alternative courses of action, the person should be dissatisfied, but stuck with the choice, because it is the best available. When outcome from chosen behavior is less than expected, but also less than expected from alternative choices, the person is likely to switch to one of the alternatives. Homans also postulated that when a person's action does not receive the reward expected or receives unexpected punishment, the person will be angry and may perform aggressive behavior. This proposition is consistent with our discussion of anger in chapter 3. Conversely, when a person's action receives as much or more reward than expected or less punishment than expected, the person will be pleased and more likely to perform approving behavior toward social partners. By the use of aggressive and approving behaviors a person can coerce or induce partners in social exchange to behave according to the person's expectations.

Expectation is an integral part of the ability to learn. We

suggested in chapter 2 that an animal compares current situations with past experience in a continual effort to anticipate rewards and punishments, to estimate outcome before it happens. Using a consistency principle, the animal assigns a current situation to a class of situations it has encountered before, and it makes *a priori* evaluations of the outcomes of various behaviors it can perform. These *a priori* evaluations are expectations of reward or punishment. As Homans said, "what a man expects to get by way of reward or punishment under a given set of circumstances (stimuli) is what he has in fact received, observed, or was told others received, under similar circumstances in the past."[5] If expectations continually fail to be met, then such experience alters future expectations.

Expectations are more general than *a priori* evaluations of outcomes. They are predictions of what will happen. We form expectations of how another person will behave, how a situation will develop or how a machine will operate. Such predictions are based on experience, either our own or someone else's, with persons, situations and machines. The cognitive trick is to find something from our experience which matches the current person, place or thing. History rarely repeats itself exactly, so the task is to find something which is similar, at least in the qualities relevant to the desired prediction. We must attribute qualities to the current object of concern so that we can say something like "All dogs I have known have barked. As this animal looks like a dog, I expect it will bark." Probability is a crucial part of expectation, so a person might also say, "Only one of the many dogs I have known has bitten me, so I expect this dog will not bite me."[6]

⚜ ⚜

We are most interested in how people make decisions when personal experience cannot predict what might happen. Confronted with an ambiguous situation, people turn to each other for cues as to how to behave. But they do not turn to just anyone. Each person refers to others who are somehow special to the person. In our discussion of fear in chapter 3, we suggested the importance of the mother in determining the infant monkey's or the human child's response to unfamiliar stimuli. The social attachment to the mother acts as an anchor or reference point for the offspring's behavioral decisions. In fact, social psychologists often use the terms *reference person* (also called *significant other*) and *reference group* in theorizing about social influence on individual decisions. The specialness of a reference person may be due to an emotional attachment of liking, respect, or dependence built up through a history of rewarding social interactions. Or the specialness may have more instrumental reasons such as the reference person's success in relevant situations, success measured as social, financial or other rewards. In some animals, the attachment and specialness may be initiated by imprinting, but most likely it is cemented by rewarding experience.

It is a common-sense notion that we tend to follow the example or advice of people we like or respect. We might sometimes think to ourselves, "If they say it is good, it is probably good." More often we just assimilate their evaluation without thinking. The specialness of a reference person may be extended to others if we see these others are special to our reference person. For example, a child uses its mother's evaluations to build up reference persons and groups. We form or change our evaluations to be consistent with our reference persons', because we want to please them so they will approve of us—an exchange of rewards.

This common-sense notion is formalized as the starting assumption of several psychological viewpoints, known collectively as cognitive consistency theories.[7] The assumption is that people perceive relations between themselves, other people, objects, and ideas as consistent or inconsistent, and that the perceiver is satisfied only with consistent perceptions. The intellectual history of this assumption starts with Fritz Heider, who is most closely associated with the branch called balance theory.[8] James A. Davis applied balance theory to a wide variety of social phenomena.[9] His approach is used here to illustrate the *P-O-X* cycle of balance theory.

The *Person* (P) is the individual whose behavior is predicted by the theory—the individual whose cognitive balance or consistency we are considering. *Other* (O) is some additional individual. *X* is some object, idea, or a third individual. We have already used linear graphs in previous chapters, so the reader should be familiar with the device. In this case (see illustration below), the lines can either refer to evaluation (liking, approval, admiration, rejection, condemnation) or to a "unit relation" between the entities, such as similarity, causality or ownership. Evaluation may be a signed value on a positive-to-negative scale. It is difficult to think of negative unit relations, but such relations clearly may vary in positive value. The net value of a line is the sum of the signed values of the various evaluations and unit relations between the two entities connected by the line. The value of the "cycle" is the product of the net values of its three lines. A cycle with a positive value is "balanced," and a cycle with a negative value is "unbalanced." People prefer balanced cycles. They react to unbalanced cycles with feelings of distress, tension or discomfort, feelings which psychologists often refer to together as cognitive dissonance. If possible, people will act to change unbalanced cycles to balanced cycles.

As Davis said, "One of the better known case studies in the marriage and family literature involves the structural

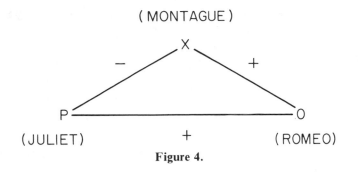

(MONTAGUE)

Figure 4.

imbalance incurred by two Veronese adolescents, Juliet Capulet and Romeo Montague. Although their families are bitter enemies, the two fall in love, and in Act II, Scene 2, Juliet muses, 'O Romeo, Romeo! wherefore art thou Romeo? . . . 'tis but thy name that is my enemy.' "[10] Which brings us to figure 4.[11] Juliet loves Romeo (strongly positive evaluation). Juliet hates Montagues (strongly negative evaluation). Romeo is a Montague (strongly positive unit relation). Notice that Juliet hates Montagues not because of anything the Montagues have done to her, but because her family (reference group) hates Montagues.

Figure 5 shows Juliet's perceptions before meeting Romeo.

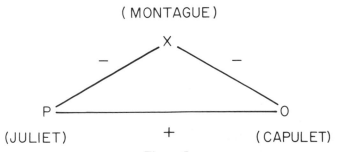

(MONTAGUE)

Figure 5.

She both loves and is part of her family. She perceives that all her family hate the Montagues. To balance her perceptions she must also hate the Montagues (the algebraic product of the signs is then positive—a balanced cycle). The crucial point to remember is that it is Juliet's *perceptions* that are interacting. If Juliet had perceived Romeo as a Montague when they first met, then it is highly unlikely that she would have fallen in love with him. Common sense tells us that, but so does balance theory. She fell in love before she knew. The unbalanced cycle was created only when she discovered Romeo's name. "My only love sprung from my only hate! Too early seen unknown, and known too late!" (Act I, Scene 5).[12]

In chapters 2 and 3 we asserted the importance of consistency in making evaluations from experience and in building chains of secondary reinforcers. In fact, we worked backward from the assumption that need for consistency is a crucial element in the cognitive structure of the human mind. It is our belief that the need for cognitive consistency is probably characteristic of any creature that refers to experience when making decisions. We find it useful to view cognitive consistency as one of several definitions of reward. In other words, learning animals are programmed to repeat behaviors that increase pleasure, reduce pain, reduce anger, reduce fear or increase cognitive consistency.

꙳

One purpose in digging out these social psychological viewpoints is to use them in understanding the reactions of humans in social groups to innovations. Concern about promotion and acceptance of new products and techniques has led to a large and diverse literature on the adoption and diffusion of innovations.[13] While this research has lacked theoretical orientation, it is invaluable for understanding why some cultural traits spread and others do not. Rural sociologists led the way in their analysis of adoption of new farming practices, such as planting of hybrid seed corn. Bryce Ryan and Neal C. Gross interviewed farmers in two Iowa communities to determine when each farmer had first heard of hybrid seed corn and then when each had first planted the new seed.[14] Figure 6 shows the accumulation of first hearings and first adoptings.[15] Actual planting lagged several years behind first hearing about the corn, showing that awareness of an innovation is not the same as deciding

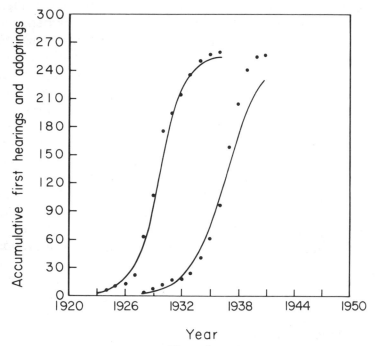

Year

Figure 6.
Accumulative first hearings and first adoptings of hybrid corn by farmers in two Iowa communities, plotted on arithmetic coordinates. The lines represent least-squares logistic equations for data from Ryan and Gross. (Figure and legend from Hamblin, Jacobsen, and Miller.)

to adopt it. The rural sociologists have come to see the adoption of an innovation as a process of decision-making divided into five stages—awareness, interest, evaluation, trial, and complete adoption. In short, a person becomes aware of an innovation, then evaluates it, then decides to adopt it or not. These three steps overlap to some extent, creating the interest and trial stages.

The logistic form of accumulation of both first hearings and adoptions indicates a facilitative interaction between the farmers. In other words, they are telling each other first what they have heard about the corn and then about their own experiences with planting the new seed. Interpersonal communication serves both to relay information and also to influence by example or active persuasion the evaluations of undecided farmers. When adoption involves some financial or social risk and information about the innovation is ambiguous, a person is more likely to adopt it if subject to influence from a trusted source, such as a farmer friend who has already adopted it (in the case of the late-adopting farmer) or the county extension agent or university expert (in the case of the early adopter).

Alex O. Thio has advanced the concept of adopter-innovation compatibility as a general explanation for variation in the rate and extent of adoption.[16] His proposition is that the more compatible the characteristics of the innovation are with the potential adopter's cultural, social, and social psychological attributes prior to its introduction, the greater are the chances of its acceptance. Once aware of an innovation, a person's evaluation of it is based on personal perception of the innovation's attributes and of how these attributes relate to people, institutions and ideas which serve as positive or negative references for the person's attitudes and behavior. For instance, if a man highly values economic profit, he is most likely to adopt an innovation perceived as profitable.

If the potential profitability is uncertain, he may wait to see if a highly respected (i.e., profit-getting) business colleague adopts the innovation. When the adoption is made, he may later find that the decision conflicts with a highly valued religious belief. If he values religion more than money, he will probably reverse his decision. But if money is more important, he will probably devalue religion in some fashion. Every adoption decision has the potential to cause changes in the value system that molded the decision. In turn, a person's adoption behavior will influence others who use this person as a reference for their attitudes and behavior.

This compatibility concept fits within the paradigms of both exchange theory and cognitive consistency theories. For example, a Catholic woman might have an abortion despite Church opposition, because she is subject to multiple influences, or multiple "cycles," which may be in competition. Let us say that the pregnant woman highly values both the Church and her current economic status. If she has the baby, her economic status goes down, so an abortion will help her maintain her economic status, but the Church opposes abortion. This dilemma is diagramed in figure 7. What will be her attitude toward abortion? She cannot balance

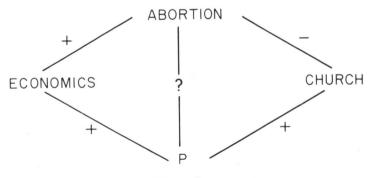

Figure 7.

both cycles, so she must decide which unbalanced state she can most easily tolerate. Is her economic status or her Church allegiance more important? This question can be rephrased as a comparison of the expected "profit" (rewards minus costs) of having an abortion versus the expected "profit" of having the child. Cognitive balance, like pleasure and freedom from pain, fear and anger, is a desired state, seldom fully achieved for long periods of time. When choosing from various courses of action, people choose the one they think will bring them closest to the desired state.

Davis used balance theory to generate a set of predictions about acceptance of innovations.[17] For instance, innovations introduced by popular or highly respected members of a group will be accepted by other members more quickly than those introduced by less liked or less respected members. Also, the greater the liking and homogeneity between group members, the more rapidly an innovation will spread through the group. The rate at which an innovation spreads from one group to another increases as the number of individuals belonging to both groups increases. If a community is polarized into two opposing factions, an innovation will spread rapidly in one faction but slowly in the other. The simple fact that the one faction introduces the innovation may be a handicap to its spread to and within the opposing faction.

The history of a Greek farming town described by Constantine A. Yeracaris well illustrates the spread of innovations within a polarized community.[18] The town was politically polarized during the 1947–1949 guerrilla war between the leftist EAM (National Liberation Front) and the relatively conservative Greek government. In early 1950, some former members of the defeated EAM organized a farmer's marketing cooperative in the town. Beyond its marketing activities, the organization probably served informally to protect its leftist membership from retribution by local conservatives supported by the government. Before the war the area's principal crop, tobacco, was planted by all farmers regardless of political affiliation. Then in late 1950, a few members of the leftist-organized cooperative planted strawberries for the first time in local history. The idea and a few plants had been brought by the son of one of the local EAM leaders. He had been living in one of the few districts in Greece where strawberries were grown. He explored the idea of strawberry cultivation with his father and his father's friends, who were also members of the local EAM leadership.

In 1951, the strawberry crop was successful beyond expectations, providing the impetus for its planting by a large proportion of the local farmers. By the end of 1956, 84 percent of the members of the cooperative were growing strawberries, while only 28 percent of the nonmember farmers were doing so. It is difficult to understand this split without knowing the history of the town. At the time strawberry cultivation was introduced there was no overt evidence of the political polarization. The history of conflict was represented in the farmers' minds as attitudes and evaluations of others. The political associations with strawberry cultivation sped its acceptance by the cooperative members, who were mainly leftists, and slowed its acceptance by others, who were mainly conservatives, even though the strawberry crop was known by all to be profitable compared to their traditional tobacco crop. Former EAM members adopting the innovation were of all ages and educational statuses, whereas conservatives who adopted were generally younger and better educated than their nonadopting conservative peers. The appeal of strawberry growing to all types of leftists was no doubt due as much to the local EAM leadership's encouragement and the consistency of agricultural innovation with the EAM's historical orientation toward social progress as to the profitability of strawberry cultivation itself. Among the conservatives, the younger, better educated farmers were the most likely to place profitability above political association. In 1957, conservatives set up their own government-supported marketing and credit cooperative, which encouraged strawberry cultivation. Eventually most conservative farmers also cultivated strawberries so that 80 percent of all the local farmers had adopted this innovation by 1966.

⤜⤛ ⤜⤛

In this and the preceding chapters, we have gone about as far as we know how or dare to go in our exploratory description of learning and decision-making. We have emphasized individual decisions regarding the adoption of innovations, because these decisions best illustrate the linkage between individual learning and the aggregate or population phenomena of cultural stability and change. The following chapters deal more directly with population phenomena, starting with a modeling approach analogous to that used by population geneticists.

CHAPTER SIX

THE MATHEMATICS OF CULTURE

> . . . ideas have retained some of the properties of organisms. Like these, they tend to perpetuate their structures and to multiply them; they too can fuse, recombine, segregate their contents; in short, they too can evolve and in this evolution selection certainly plays a role. I shall not hazard a theory of the selection of ideas.
>
> —JACQUES MONOD[1]

The mathematical theory of genetical evolution began with the monumental works of Sir Ronald Fisher, J. B. S. Haldane and Sewall Wright in the 1920s and 1930s.[2] By contrast, fifty years later the mathematical theory of cultural evolution is still in its infancy. In 1973, two Stanford University biologists, Luigi Cavalli-Sforza and Marcus Feldman, published the first in a series of articles on mathematical models of cultural inheritance.[3] To incorporate the essence of cultural evolution into a mathematical model is, to say the least, a bold proposition. Yet, we agree with Cavalli-Sforza that "whenever an observation is quantifiable it can be the object of a mathematical theory."[4] This chapter is designed to illustrate the different forms these models may take and a variety of their potential applications. In chapter 7, we shall apply a very simple model of cultural inheritance to an important issue raised by sociobiologists in their attempts to apply genetic models to human behavior.

The aim of a mathematical theory of culture is to explain the evolution of learned traits such as ideas, technologies, social customs and languages. The basic sources of new ideas, customs, and so forth, are innovation and diffusion from other groups. New traits spread by social learning from individual to individual and, thus, from generation to generation. In most of the models, culturally transmitted traits are represented in individuals as continuous phenotypic variables. In this regard, the traits are like the evaluations discussed throughout this book; both are represented as signed values on a continuous positive-to-negative scale. Evaluations change as a result of individual experience and we suggest that the Cavalli-Sforza and Feldman models capture the essence of how evaluations change as a result of social learning.

୶ଏ୭ ଡ଼ଏ୬

In their simplest models, Cavalli-Sforza and Feldman considered only cultural inheritance between generations.[5] The phenotype ($\phi_{i,t}$) of individual i in generation t is assumed to represent a weighted mean of the phenotypes ($\phi_{j,t-1}$) of certain individuals in the parental generation plus a random variable E_i determined by the experience of individual i. This is expressed by the model

$$\phi_{i,t} = \sum_{j=1}^{N} w_{i,j}\phi_{j,t-1} + E_i. \tag{6.1}$$

The terms $w_{i,j}$ sum to unity and each term represents the relative influence of an individual in the parental generation on the phenotype of individual i. The model implies Lamarckian inheritance, but is that not the essence of cultural evolution? Individuals *acquire* the phenotypes of the parental generation and pass these acquired traits on to the next generation. Of course, in every society, some individuals, perhaps parents, teachers and priests, exert a strong influence while others have little or no influence. The relative influences of different individuals are reflected in the model by the relative weights, $w_{i,j}$, assigned to them.

The temperature at which a cake is baked is an example of a continuous phenotypic variable since modern ovens can be set at any temperature up to about 500°F. Ignoring for now the influence of recipe books, most people initially learn the proper temperature to bake a cake from the suggestions of friends and relatives, and the temperature adopted may be expected, on the average, to be the weighted mean of the suggested temperatures. Still the actual temperature eventually adopted by an individual will not be exactly this weighted mean but will deviate from the mean because of random variation in the learning process. By chance an individual may not hear the opinion of a respected friend or may have a cake fall because a door is slammed but blame the failure on the baking temperature. In the Cavalli-Sforza and Feldman models, these unpredictable influences are included in the random variable E_i. Cavalli-Sforza and Feldman[6] assumed that E_i is normally distributed with mean zero and variance σ^2. We call σ^2 the *learning variance*. The assumption of a mean of zero simply means these random influences are equally likely to increase or decrease the phenotype. Throughout our discussion we assume no genetic variance in phenotypes.

In the simplest models group size (N) is considered constant and each individual is assumed to have one offspring which replaces it as individual i in the next generation. The weighting factors, $w_{i,j}$, for all N individuals can thus be written as a matrix of the form

$$\mathbf{W} = \begin{bmatrix} w_{1,1} & w_{1,2} & \cdots & w_{1,N} \\ w_{2,1} & w_{2,2} & \cdots & w_{2,N} \\ \vdots & \vdots & & \vdots \\ w_{N,1} & w_{N,2} & \cdots & w_{N,N} \end{bmatrix}.$$

Assuming that the random variables E_i are independent both within and between generations, the phenotypes of generation t can be extrapolated from those of their parental generation, $t - 1$, by the equation

$$\phi_t = W\phi_{t-1} + E,$$

where ϕ_t, ϕ_{t-1}, and E are column vectors. Furthermore, since the mean of the random variable E_i is zero, the expected value of ϕ_t is

$$E(\phi_t) = W\phi_{t-1} = W^t\phi_0, \tag{6.2}$$

where ϕ_0 is the initial phenotype vector, t generations ago.[7]

In many animal species and some human societies, infant contact is much greater with one parent, usually the mother, than with all other adults. In this case the societal contributions to an infant's behavior can be partitioned into the parental influence $(1 - g)$ and the influence of the rest of the social group (g). A model corresponding to equation 6.1 can thus be written as

$$\phi_{i,t} = (1 - g)\, \phi_{p,t-1} + g\bar{\phi}_{t-1} + E_i, \tag{6.3}$$

where $\phi_{p,t-1}$ is the parent's phenotype and $\bar{\phi}_{t-1}$ is the average phenotype in the parental generation.[8] This case is particularly easy to analyze since the corresponding transmission matrix (W) is doubly stochastic (i.e., $\Sigma_{i=1}^{N} w_{i,j} = 1 = \Sigma_{j=1}^{N} w_{i,j}$). For such a doubly stochastic transmission matrix, the *expected* mean phenotype does not change between generations; that is,

$$E(\bar{\phi}_t) = \bar{\phi}_{t-1}. \tag{6.4}$$

Still the mean phenotype may undergo *random cultural drift* because of the random variable E_i. The magnitude of such drift can be expressed as the expected mean square difference between the original mean phenotype $(\bar{\phi}_0)$ and the mean phenotype after t generations. In this case the expected mean square difference is

$$E(\bar{\phi}_t - \bar{\phi}_0)^2 = t\sigma^2/N. \tag{6.5}$$

Equation 6.5 states that cultural drift increases with time and is greatest in small groups.[9] In a very large group, random cultural drift may be negligible.

Equation 6.5 indicates that the mean of a culturally determined phenotype will drift about with time, but how variable will the phenotype be during any one generation? The within-generation phenotypic variance is calculated by the equation

$$V_t = E\left[\frac{\sum_{i=1}^{N} (\phi_{i,t} - \bar{\phi}_t)^2}{N - 1}\right] = (1 - g)^2 V_{t-1} + \sigma^2. \tag{6.6}$$

After many generations this variance reaches an asymptotic value[10] given by

$$V_\infty = \frac{\sigma^2}{1 - (1 - g)^2}. \tag{6.7}$$

Thus, if there is no group influence (i.e., $g = 0$), the variance is unbounded and continues to increase indefinitely. Still, any group influence, however slight, sets a finite upper bound to phenotypic variance. At the extreme of no parental influence and complete group influence (i.e., $g = 1$), the asymptotic variance is simply the learning variance, σ^2. Stated more simply, parental influence promotes cultural diversity.

Cavalli-Sforza and Feldman showed that the asymptotic distribution of phenotypes is normal with the expected variance given by equation 6.7 and with an expected mean equal to the initial mean $\bar{\phi}_0$.[11] This is illustrated by figure 8. The distribution of phenotypes in any one generation is normal with expected variance V_∞, but the mean of the distribution drifts at random around the expected value of $\bar{\phi}_0$.

❧ ☙

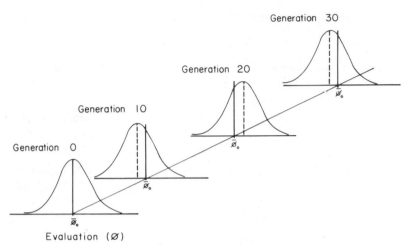

Figure 8.
The distribution of evaluations in a population may undergo random cultural drift. The distribution is asymptotically normal with a variance determined by both learning error and social group influence. The mean evaluation $(\overline{\phi}_t)$ drifts randomly around the initial mean $(\overline{\phi}_o)$.

We have suggested that the phenotypes of the Cavalli-Sforza and Feldman models may be used to represent socially influenced evaluations of behavioral options. For example, the phenotype could represent attitudes towards an innovation and an individual might only accept the innovation if his evaluation were positive. The initial evaluations (ϕ_0) of an innovation are determined by both individual reinforcement experience and by social influence. Extrapolating from these evaluations to the next generation brings up two complications. First, individuals may change their evaluations within a single generation though the models assume fixed evaluations. We shall deal with this problem shortly. Second, an individual's Darwinian fitness may depend critically on the individual's evaluation; for example, an individual's chances of surviving to influence the next generation may depend on whether or not an innovation is adopted. Figure 9 illus-

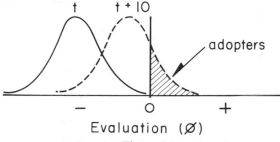

t   t + 10

adopters

—   O   +

Evaluation (∅)

Figure 9.
Individuals only adopt an innovation if their evaluations of it are positive.
Random cultural drift alone can result in some individuals adopting a
previously rejected innovation.

trates how the Cavalli-Sforza and Feldman models can be applied when fitness varies with phenotype.

Many species of wild mushrooms are very poisonous, and accordingly, most humans are quite reluctant to eat unidentified mushrooms, because of cultural accumulation of bad experiences. Relatively few people have actually eaten poisonous mushrooms; still the negative attitudes persist from generation to generation. The attitudes persist because children learn from adults not to eat wild mushrooms, but, alas, children do not learn exactly what they are told. Because of learning variance, attitudes towards eating wild mushrooms may vary; indeed they may show the kind of random cultural drift shown in figure 8. As the attitudes drift toward the positive end of the evaluation scale, some individuals are likely to try wild mushrooms (see figure 9). If a mushroom taster becomes ill but lives to tell, both he and his friend might devalue mushroom eating. But what if the mushroom taster always dies, and furthermore, the cause of death is unknown to the rest of society? One individual's bad luck will not then affect the attitudes of other individuals of his generation. But might it not affect the attitudes of future generations?

Let us analyze the problem using the model given by equation 6.3. The taster's death does not affect the attitudes of others in his own generation, but it does lower the mean phenotype ($\overline{\phi}_{t-1}$) of the parental generation since the taster had a positive evaluation and died. If the group size (N) is small and the group influence (g) large, the death of one individual with a high evaluation may significantly lower the evaluations learned by the next generation, even though the cause of death is unknown. If, on the other hand, the group influence is small, then the taster's death has little effect on the next generation except for that on his own children. If the taster dies before reproducing, then he does not pass his own positive evaluation on to his children. If the taster dies after reproducing and influencing his own children, then his children will acquire his high evaluation of eating mushrooms and are likely to poison themselves. The net effect is the same—a systematic pressure that selects against eating mushrooms. This is an example of *cultural selection*.[12]

The Cavalli-Sforza and Feldman models can be readily applied to within-generation cultural diffusion by redefining the elements ($w_{i,j}$) of the transmission matrix.[13] In equation 6.1, the term $w_{i,j}$ was defined as the influence of individual j in the parental generation on the phenotype of individual i in the next generation. In the case of uniparental inheritance, $w_{i,j} = 1 - g$ was simply the influence of the parent on its own offspring's phenotype. Equation 6.1 can represent within-generation diffusion by considering the phenotype of each individual at different times. The individuals in the group remain the same, but their phenotypes change periodically under the influence of other group members and personal experience. For example, if the phenotypes are attitudes toward female birth control pills, then after each time segment, each woman is assumed to reevaluate her attitude based on her previous attitude, on her recent experience, and on the attitudes of other women in her social group. Since $w_{i,j}$ is defined as the relative influence of individual j on the attitude of individual i, $w_{i,i}$ is a measure of the tendency of an individual *not* to change her own attitude.

In the Cavalli-Sforza and Feldman models, the terms $w_{i,j}$ of the transmission matrix measure the influence of one individual on the attitudes of another. There may be a lot of variation in these terms due, in particular, to variability in the frequency of contact between individuals and to the sequence of contact. Often an individual will accept an innovation based on the evaluation of only one or a few friends and later reject it based on a larger sample of evaluations. For example, a youngster may try LSD, because some friends do, but later reject it when he finds that most people disapprove. Many fads that fizzle may fall into this general category. Each individual may be thought of as an opinion poll starting with an initial evaluation based on individual reinforcement history. As each individual polls the opinions of others, his own evaluation changes. Even if most initial evaluations are overwhelmingly negative, the fad may catch on in isolated pockets where, by chance, initial evaluations are high. As individuals in these pockets expand their opinion samples they too may reject the innovation, in which case the fad dies out.

To illustrate how evaluations may change in social groups, we consider the attitudes of three interacting individuals toward the acceptance of an innovation. For simplicity, we assume the learning error (σ^2) is zero, so changes in evaluations are only based on social influences. Consider first how attitudes change if the transmission matrix is

$$\mathbf{W} = \begin{bmatrix} 1.0 & 0.0 & 0.0 \\ 0.2 & 0.8 & 0.0 \\ 0.0 & 0.2 & 0.8 \end{bmatrix}.$$

In this case all three attitudes will converge to that originally held only by individual 1. This is because individual 1 is not influenced by the other two individuals, but he influences their attitudes. Compare this to the case were the transmission matrix is

$$\mathbf{W} = \begin{bmatrix} 0.8 & 0.1 & 0.1 \\ 0.1 & 0.8 & 0.1 \\ 0.1 & 0.1 & 0.8 \end{bmatrix}.$$

Here, no one individual dominates the others, and eventually the attitudes of all three converge to the mean of the original attitudes. If the original mean is positive, eventually all three individuals accept the innovation; if the original mean is negative, all three eventually reject it. The speed of convergence in attitudes is inversely proportional to the diagonal terms, $w_{i,i}$, since these measure the tendency of each individual not to change his attitude.

Finally, consider the outcome when the matrix is

$$\mathbf{W} = \begin{bmatrix} 0.3 & 0.0 & 0.7 \\ 0.7 & 0.3 & 0.0 \\ 0.0 & 0.7 & 0.3 \end{bmatrix}.$$

In this example, too, all attitudes eventually converge to the original mean attitude. However, it is unlike the last example in that here the attitudes may oscillate as they approach their common goal. For example, imagine that originally individual 1 accepts the innovation (say $\phi_{1,0} = +1$), individual 2 is neutral (i.e., $\phi_{2,0} = 0$) and individual 3 rejects it (say $\phi_{3,0} = -1$). Then after just one time period, individual 2 will accept the innovation because of his high evaluation of individual 1's attitude, which was originally positive. However, in the meantime, individual 1 has also changed his mind and now rejects the innovation because of his high evaluation of individual 3, originally a rejector. So round and round the evaluations go, only to converge, in the end, on the original mean attitude, which is neutral. How very human a matrix!

✿ ✿

So far we have considered social learning to be an averaging process and the phenotypes to be continuous variables. However, many behavioral traits which might be transmitted culturally are not easily represented as continuous phenotypic variables. For example, an individual either accepts or rejects an innovation, and even though potential attitudes are continuous, no middle ground is easily discerned by an observer. The Cavalli-Sforza and Feldman models can be modified to account for the transmission of discrete traits by redefining the elements of the transmission matrices. Equation 6.1 can be modified to read

$$\phi_{i,t} = \sum_{j=1}^{N} \delta_{i,j}\phi_{j,t-1}, \tag{6.8}$$

where

$$\delta_{i,j} = \begin{cases} 1 & \text{if individual } i \text{ adopts its phenotype} \\ & \text{from individual } j \\ 0 & \text{otherwise.} \end{cases}$$

The terms of the transmission matrix are also redefined as

$$w_{i,j} = \text{Prob}[\delta_{i,j} = 1].$$

What this means is that individual i adopts the particular attitude of one individual of the parental generation, rather than adopting an intermediate or averaged attitude. The terms $w_{i,j}$ give the probability that the particular attitude adopted is that of individual j. For convenience, we assume no learning error except as results from the stochastic nature of who learns from whom.

One advantage of modeling the transmission of *discrete* traits is that individuals may not need to be treated separately but instead may be place in a few categories, such as adopters and nonadopters of an innovation. If the probability that an individual changes phenotype (i.e., adopter to nonadopter or nonadopter to adopter) depends solely on his current phenotype and on the number of individuals in each of two phenotypic categories, then a 2 × 2 transmission matrix will describe the dynamics of the entire population. For example, assume that a population can be divided into $n_{1,t}$ adopters, and $n_{2,t}$ nonadopters at time t, so that $n_{1,t} + n_{2,t} = N_t$ is the size of the entire population. Furthermore, assume that once an adopter, always an adopter (ie., $w_{1,1} = 1$ and $w_{1,2} = 0$) and that in each time interval nonadopters become adopters with probability p. The complete transmission matrix is then

$$\mathbf{W} = \begin{bmatrix} 1 & 0 \\ 1 - p & p \end{bmatrix}.$$

The expected number of adopters at time t is simply

$$E(n_{1,t}) = n_{1,t-1} + pn_{2,t-1}, \tag{6.9}$$

which is positive so long as there are some nonadopters left. So eventually every one adopts the innovation and the rate of convergence just depends on how many nonadopters are left.

Even if an innovation will eventually be accepted by everybody, there is no particular reason why the probability of adoption should be constant. For example, the probability of adoption might be a function of the number of previous adopters. In many fads the probability of adoption initially rises and then declines as more and more people adopt the innovation. For a very rewarding innovation which is eventually adopted by everyone, adoption may simply depend on hearing about the innovation or seeing it, in which case, the probability of adoption will increase as the number of adopters increases. This gives rise to a frequency-dependent process where the number of adopters is given by an equation of the form

$$E(n_{1,t}) = n_{1,t-1} + kn_{1,t-1}n_{2,t-1}. \tag{6.10}$$

Equation 6.10 is called a logistic equation, according to which the number of adopters initially increases slowly, then accelerates and finally levels out after most of the population has adopted the innovation. The primary difference between equations 6.9 and 6.10 is that only in the latter does the probability of adoption change with the number of adopters. Clearly then, equation 6.10 may be more appropriate when individuals interact, and equation 6.9 more appropriate when they do not.

James S. Coleman and his colleagues compared the cultural diffusion of a new prescription drug in four midwestern American communities.[14] An earlier study had classified the local physicians as either integrated or isolated depending on the social and professional interactions they had with other doctors. Coleman reasoned that the diffusion of the drug innovation among the integrated physicians would be better described by a logistic equation and that the diffusion among isolated physicians would be better described by

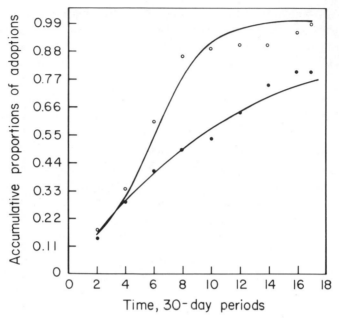

Figure 10.
Accumulative adoptions of a new drug for prescriptions by integrated physicians (open points) and isolated physicians (solid points), plotted on arithmetic coordinates by time. The lines represent logistic and decaying exponential equations, which Coleman fitted to the data. (Figure and legend from Hamblin, Jacobsen, and Miller.)

equation 6.9. This would be the case if the integrated physicians learned of the drug primarily from one another, but the isolated physicians learned of it primarily from a constant external source, such as professional journals or advertisements from distributors. The results are shown in figure 10 and seem to support Coleman's claim.[15]

≈⁂≈ ≈⁂≈

In chapter 4, we outlined a positive feedback system whereby social learning leads to formation of cliques or factions within social groups. The lack of communication between factions may retard the diffusion of an innovation between them, even though one faction has found the innovation very rewarding. In chapter 5, we related the story of a polarized Greek community in which strawberry growing was quickly adopted by leftist farmers, who found the new crop very profitable. Nonetheless, the innovation was slow to spread to politically conservative farmers. Conservative farmers devalued strawberry farming because they associated it with the leftists. Of course, left and right are only relative terms. Some moderate conservatives no doubt saw the profits of moderate leftists and accepted the innovation, because their devaluation of it was small relative to their evaluation of the perceived rewards. Once a few moderate conservatives accepted the innovation, it was more likely to spread to other conservatives.

The evaluation of strawberry growing could be represented as the continuous phenotypic variable in a within-generation version of the model given by equation 6.1 which considers the simultaneous evaluations of all individuals in the population. However, the essence of the dynamics of the diffusion process can be represented more simply by the somewhat artificial division of the entire population into the following four categories:

n_1, the leftist adopters,
n_2, the leftist nonadopters,
n_3, the conservative adopters,
n_4, the conservative nonadopters.

This division assumes that all leftists are equally left and that all conservatives are equally right. A model based on this division further assumes that diffusion depends only on communication and that communication is much more likely within than between factions. These assumptions are valid, as a first approximation, if the community is very polarized, and the perceived rewards of the innovation eventually outweigh political considerations. The model embodies these assumptions in the following equations for the probability $p(\mathbf{n})$ of a leftist farmer switching from tobacco to strawberries and $q(\mathbf{n})$ of a conservative farmer making the same switch:

$$p(\mathbf{n}) = n_1 N^{-1} + \beta n_3 N^{-1}$$

and

$$q(\mathbf{n}) = n_3 N^{-1} + \beta n_1 N^{-1},$$

where β is small so as to indicate little communication between the two political factions. Assuming that the rewards of strawberry growing are sufficient to prevent any reversals of the adoption decisions, the full transmission matrix is

$$\mathbf{W} = \begin{bmatrix} 1 & 0 & 0 & 0 \\ p(\mathbf{n}) & 1 - p(\mathbf{n}) & 0 & 0 \\ 0 & 0 & 1 & 0 \\ 0 & 0 & 1 - q(\mathbf{n}) & q(\mathbf{n}) \end{bmatrix}.$$

Among other things, the model predicts that the innovation would have spread more rapidly among conservative farmers than among leftist farmers had it been the former who had introduced the innovation.

   This mathematical model may contribute little to our understanding of the Greek case history, beyond what we already knew intuitively or from common sense. However, the exercise is valuable, because it shows that mathematical treatment can produce predictions that accord with common sense. This small success increases our confidence that mathematical modeling can yield useful predictions about more complex problems in the diffusion of innovations, problems that may not be so susceptible to intuitive analysis.

The purpose of this chapter has been to demonstrate that the phenomena of cultural stability and change are susceptible to moderately formal mathematical treatment, much like the treatment of problems in population genetics. However, given the present uncertain knowledge of mechanisms in cultural evolution, we recognize that such theoretical approaches may not yet be useful in thinking about interesting, controversial questions. In the next chapter, we will present a less formal way of approaching some of these interesting questions.

CHAPTER SEVEN

THE EVOLUTION OF IDEAS

Whether the scientific sociobiology will succeed in its ambition of incorporating the human sciences depends largely on the fate of its theory of kin selection. —MARSHALL SAHLINS[1]

Ideas evolve within a person's mind and within a society of interacting minds. In thinking about the evolution of ideas we find it helpful to distinguish the mental repertoire of *ideas* from the performing repertoire of *behaviors*. At the end of chapter 4, we pointed out that a distinction can be made between the repertoire of behaviors which are actually performed and a potentially much larger repertoire of behaviors, at least once observed and perhaps performed, which are remembered and held in the mind. The mental repertoire, of course, includes the performing repertoire. In most animals, only the performing repertoire can be passed on to subsequent generations, because such animals can learn from other animals only by observing actual performances. Linguistic ability allows humans to label the behaviors in the mental repertoire and pass on knowledge of them through speech (and relatively recently by writing) to other people who have never performed the behaviors nor seen them performed.

Ideas are the elements of the mental repertoire. The adoption, retention, evaluation and elimination of ideas probably follow only the rules of cognitive consistency. We make this assertion not so much because of overwhelming empirical evidence, although the psychological evidence marshaled by proponents of cognitive consistency theories (see chapter 5) is strong. The more important reason is that the assertion fits well with our view of the mental processes involved in learning. The reader can see the operation of cognitive consistency in the development of our ideas throughout this book.

We believe that ideas evolve on two distinct levels. First, ideas are accepted or rejected because they are either consistent or inconsistent with other ideas. This is not to say that people never harbor inconsistent ideas but only that people are bothered by inconsistencies and act to reduce them. Second, in attempting to make their actions consistent with their ideas, people sometimes act in ways that affect their chances to survive and propagate their ideas. Ideas disappear either because they become inconsistent with other ideas or because they motivate maladaptive behaviors.[2]

Ideas and behaviors interact closely. On one hand, observed behaviors can be the source of new ideas. On the other hand, new ideas can motivate new behaviors which can be observed and so on. Furthermore, these new behaviors can affect the Darwinian fitness of their adopters. To illustrate this interaction and its evolutionary significance, we will briefly discuss the possible origins of diversity in human ideas about residence, marriage, kinship and inheritance.

ↄ🙰ↄ ᧕🙰᧕

Starting with a mother and her children as the basic social unit, anthropologist Robin Fox, in his book *Kinship and Marriage*, examined the logical possibilities for building up larger kinship groups.[3] If the children are both male and female, the basic unit could expand by self-perpetuation— the brothers could impregnate their sisters who would then produce new recruits. However, no human society regularly follows this practice. The brothers and sisters must usually find mates outside their basic unit. This necessity creates a tension between the husband-wife bond, which tends to pull people away from their natal group, and the bond between siblings, which tends to maintain the natal group's integrity as a social unit. One logical solution is to keep the brothers and sisters together in their mother's household—a *consanguineal household*—and let the sisters establish liaisons with "visiting husbands" from other nearby households. Fox called the resulting residence pattern *natolocal*, meaning that the "spouses" stay in their natal homes even after marriage.[4] No matter how logical, it is very rare for brothers and sisters to reside together as adults. The most exemplary of the few instances is the system of the Nayar of Malabar in southwest India.[5]

The Nayar were a warrior caste, the men usually spending some time away from home as full-time soldiers. When the men completed their military service, they would return home to live with their mothers, brothers and sisters. There was a form of marriage, but it did not require either men or women to leave their natal homes. As Fox explains, before women "reached puberty they were 'married' to a man of a lineage with which their natal lineage had a special relationship. This 'marriage' was then dissolved and the woman was free to take as many as twelve 'lovers' or temporary husbands. . . . These men had visiting rights with their 'wives', and if one of the men on visiting found another's spear or shield outside the house, then he would go away and try again the next night."[6]

The Ashanti of Ghana are also natolocal. However, marriage is somewhat more institutionalized than among the Nayar. "Any evening in an Ashanti town, . . . one will see children running between the houses carrying dishes and bowls of food. They are taking it from the mother's house to the father's house. The father will be at home with his mother, and his sisters and their children."[7] In a strictly biological sense, an Ashanti woman exchanges food for sexual and other favors of her husband. But why all the bother? Would it not be much easier to make the same exchanges at home with her brothers?

One of the few things common to virtually all known human societies is that matings among close kin are discouraged. Even among the Nayar, though a woman lived with her brothers and they supported her children, they could not be among her lovers. This is not to say that incestuous matings never occur among humans; indeed, the evidence for the harmful consequence of incest comes from numerous violations of the normal rule. In one recent study, of 161 children born to women who had sexual relations with their brothers, fathers or sons, more than 40 percent had various mental or physical defects. In contrast, of 95 children born of non-incestuous matings by *the same women*, none had serious mental deficiencies and only five suffered any apparent physical abnormality.[8]

The very fact that such large numbers of children born from incestuous matings are available for scientific analysis indicates to us that active prohibition might be necessary to prevent far more incestuous matings. Natolocal residence patterns may be rare because sibling incest occurs despite prohibition. Probably the idea "incest is bad" is taught from an early age and becomes a basic idea with which other ideas and customs must be made consistent. Until recently the scientific evidence for the deleterious effects of human inbreeding was scarce and controversial. If even twentieth century scientists disagree about the harmful consequences of incest, why have people in so many societies discouraged it without the benefit of scientific evidence?

Ideas can disappear by a process similar to that of genetic natural selection. We call this process *natural subtraction* to emphasize that it is a means by which ideas are eliminated from societies. Natural subtraction is blind in the sense that societies need not "figure out" that a custom is deleterious in order for it to disappear. Consider the following hypothetical example of how natural subtraction might work in an Ashanti-like society where children grow up in consanguineal households. The children are exposed primarily to the ideas of their mother and her siblings. Since these adults grew up together, they learned similar ideas. As a result, the children of the household are likely to learn from adults who agree on most issues, and so ideas are passed faithfully within families from generation to generation.

As in any society, innovations can arise, and children are likely to learn the innovations of their parents. Suppose the adult members of a single Ashanti-like household decided that a woman's brother could also be her lover. Children of the first incestuous matings would probably be normal. However, after several generations of incest, the incidence of malformed children would be high, and the adults would also be physically and mentally less capable of providing for the children. Inevitably, the family would be unable to perpetuate itself, and the custom would decline along with the family itself.

This is not the only possible scenario. Perhaps someone would see that the custom of incest led to malformed children and would persuade the family members to change their ideas about incest. In this case, the custom would cease because the ideas which motivated it would be shown to be inconsistent with desired goals of the individuals. At any rate, whether by cognitive inconsistency or by natural subtraction, the custom would decline and eventually disappear.

An Ashanti-like society was good for our hypothetical example, because the children would be likely to learn mainly, if not solely, from adults who shared similar ideas and customs. In most societies marriage means that children are brought up by parents who grew up in different families. With the exchange of spouses between families, ideas are also exchanged. This and the many other factors which promote exchange of ideas between families means that societies become more nearly homogeneous in their ideas, and as a result, the unit of natural subtraction is raised from the family to the entire society. The natural subtraction of entire groups from societies is the main topic of the next chapter. For now we return to the evolution of ideas about kinship.

As noted earlier, in the vast majority of human societies, brothers and sisters do not normally reside together as adults. If one sex remains in the natal household, the other sex moves elsewhere upon marriage. For example, brothers often act together with their father and his brothers as an economic team, so they tend to live together. In this and other cases, when a man and woman marry, they take up residence in or near the household of the father or some other important elder male kinsman of the husband. This residence pattern is called *patrilocal*, meaning that the couple on marriage lives with the husband's father.[9] A more general term is *virilocal*, meaning residence with the husband's group, but we prefer to use the less obscure term, patrilocal. Patrilocal residence groups may contain three or more generations of brothers, linked through father-son-grandson relationships. Sisters of the brothers are, in effect, exchanged for wives from other groups.

Patrilocal residence groups are *de facto patrilineal* in that new members are recruited only through males. Similarly, the natolocal residence groups formed among the Nayar and

Ashanti are *de facto matrilineal*, as new members are recruited only through females.[10] We say *de facto* rather than *de jure*, because patriliny and matriliny are kinship ideologies rather than observable residential arrangements. Patrilocal groups become *de jure* patrilineal only when group members claim that they share membership because of descent from a common male ancestor. Then they have a patrilineal ideology, which will tend to maintain their patrilocal residence pattern.

Though the residence arrangement may have spawned the kinship ideology, the ideology has an internal logic which can become almost independent of residence arrangements. For example, reckoning all male and female descendants of a common male ancestor as members of the same kinship group means that such kinship groups cannot be the same as residence groups. The sisters of a kinship group have gone to other residential groups as wives, and the wives of a kinship group are not members even though they join the residence groups. In *de facto* groups based solely on residence, sisters would be lost from their natal groups and adopted by the residence groups of their husbands. The internal logic of most patrilineal ideologies continues to recognize the sisters as members with rights in and obligations to their natal groups even after they have joined other residential groups. Notice that the Ashanti and Nayar systems of natolocal matriliny do not generate such internal discrepancies between ideology and residence, since the kinship group maintains its integrity as a residential unit.

Once ideas about residence and kinship become institutionalized, they become basic "facts" with which other ideas, such as those about the inheritance of wealth or property rights and the choice of marriage partners, must be made consistent. Ideas about residence, marriage, kinship and inheritance tend to interlock in an internally consistent ideology. We might say these ideas conform to a cultural logic. We wonder if this cultural logic conforms to genetic logic. In other words, we ask whether such ideologies produce behaviors which maintain or increase Darwinian fitness. To pursue an answer, we must first briefly introduce the concept of inclusive fitness as used by sociobiologists.

cℋ℺ ℺ℋ℺

   William D. Hamilton published two papers in 1964 jointly entitled "The Genetical Theory of Social Behaviour."[11] The premise of the papers was simple: all genetic relatives, both descendant and nondescendant, represent avenues of potential genetic reproduction. From this notion of inclusive fitness, Hamilton concluded that the willingness of one individual to sacrifice its own Darwinian fitness for the benefit of another should be proportional to their genetic coefficient of relationship, which is defined as the probability that two alleles of the same gene in different individuals are identical by virtue of descent from a common ancestor. (Years earlier, J. B. S. Haldane had reached the same conclusion as indicated by his remark that he would be willing to lay down his own life for more than two brothers, four nephews or eight cousins.)[12] Hamilton has been very successful in showing that his theory of kin selection accounts for many aspects of the social behavior of insects, particularly the behavior of the sterile caste of social hymenoptera (bees, wasps and ants). More recently, some sociobiologists have tried to show that this kin-selection theory can explain many characteristics of human social behavior.[13]

   Haldane figured that he could actually increase his genetic contribution to future generations by sacrificing his own life (and chances to have children) to save more than eight cousins, because cousins share on average one-eighth of their genes by common descent. However, Haldane was wrong unless the wives of his male kinsmen were strictly faithful to their husbands. As Richard D. Alexander has argued, maternity is obvious; paternity can only be assumed.[14] Sexually faithful parents share one-half of their genes with their children. An unfaithful wife still shares one-half of her genes with her child regardless of who actually fathered the child, but her husband shares either none or one-half of his genes with the child. If paternity is uncertain, the expected number of genes the father shares with the child is one-half times the probability that he fathered the child. Table 7.1 shows the genetic coefficients of relationship of various relatives assuming that a society can be characterized by a reliability parameter R, which is the probability that fathers, in general, sire their wives' children. Notice that the unreliability of paternity creates asymmetries in kinship for categories that we equate in English. For example, individuals that we call cousins are not necessarily equally related to us. If the reliability of paternity was less than certain ($R = 1$) in Victorian England, we would expect Haldane's genes to have fared better had he sacrificed himself for eight children of his mother's sister than for eight children of his father's brother.

As Alexander has pointed out, if reliability of paternity is low, a man may actually be more related genetically to his sisters' children than to the children of his own wife.[15] This is apparent in table 7.1 when the reliability of paternity is below about 0.3. A man can expect, in the probabilistic sense, to share at least one-eighth of his genes with his sisters' children but he cannot be certain of sharing any genes with his wife's children. Thus, in a society with low reliability of paternity, genetic logic would lead a man to favor his sisters' children over his own wife's children because in doing so he can increase his genetic contribution to future generations.

Table 7.1. Genetic Coefficients of Relationship.

Between Relatives of Different Generations

Reliability of Paternity	Mother and Child	Father and Child	Person and Sister's Child	Person and Brother's Child
R	$\frac{1}{2}$	$\frac{1}{2}R$	$\frac{1}{8} + \frac{1}{8}R^2$	$\frac{1}{8}R + \frac{1}{8}R^3$
0.0	0.500	0.000	0.125	0.000
0.2	0.500	0.100	0.130	0.026
0.4	0.500	0.200	0.145	0.058
0.6	0.500	0.300	0.170	0.102
0.8	0.500	0.400	0.205	0.164
1.0	0.500	0.500	0.250	0.250

Between Relatives of the Same Generation

Reliability of Paternity	Siblings	Cousins Related by 2 Sisters	Cousins Related by Brother and Sister	Cousins Related by 2 Brothers
R	$\frac{1}{4} + \frac{1}{4}R^2$	$\frac{1}{16} + \frac{1}{16}R^2$	$\frac{1}{16}R + \frac{1}{16}R^3$	$\frac{1}{16}R^2 + \frac{1}{16}R^4$
0.0	0.250	0.062	0.000	0.000
0.2	0.260	0.065	0.013	0.003
0.4	0.290	0.072	0.029	0.012
0.6	0.340	0.085	0.051	0.031
0.8	0.410	0.102	0.082	0.066
1.0	0.500	0.125	0.125	0.125

In most societies, men who accumulate material wealth during their own lives eventually pass the wealth on to children of the next generation. Which children inherit this wealth varies from society to society. In natolocal societies, such as the Ashanti and the Nayar, marriage ties are loose, making paternity uncertain. In accord with kin-selection theory, in natolocal societies men usually pass wealth to their sisters' children rather than to their own wives' children. In patrilocal societies, marriage ties are relatively strong, making reliability of paternity relatively high. Again in accord with genetic logic, men in patrilocal societies pass wealth to the children of their wives rather than those of their sisters.

⚜︎ ⚜︎

We have an alternative explanation for the observed associations of inheritance ideas and residence patterns.[16] The basis of sociobiological theory is that genes cause people to behave in certain ways that, in turn, perpetuate those genes from generation to generation. We propose that ideas can motivate people to behave in certain ways that, in turn, perpetuate those ideas from generation to generation. Our starting assumption is taken from the discussion of cognitive consistency theory in chapter 5. We assume that the more ideas two people share, the more they will like each other, and therefore, the more they will affiliate, cooperate and reciprocate. In essence people will tend to propagate their own ideas by helping other people who have similar ideas. In this view, people should be willing to help kin more than nonkin, because kin learn similar ideas from common ancestors and *not* because kin share similar genes.

Consider the following informal cultural model, which makes some quantitative predictions that differ from the predictions of the genetic models of sociobiology. Imagine that ideas, like genes, are particulate and that children inherit their ideas by learning from their parents. If a child's parents have different ideas on a particular issue, let us say that a child learns the father's idea with probability P and learns the mother's idea with probability M. Then, the probability that two siblings learn the same idea from the same parent is $P^2 + M^2$, which is the probability they both learn from their father plus the probability they both learn from their mother.[17] This is the probability of cultural identity by descent and can be called the *cultural coefficient of relationship*. Like the genetic coefficient of relationship, the cultural coefficient can be calculated for any pair of relatives. In fact, when paternity is certain and learning is equal and entirely from the two parents ($P = M = \frac{1}{2}$), the cultural coefficients are identical to the genetic coefficients for all pairs of relatives.

Table 7.2 shows the cultural coefficients of relationship for the same pairs of relatives as in table 7.1 but for different degrees of maternal versus paternal influence over learning (assuming $P + M = 1$). When children are equally likely to learn from either parent ($P = M = \frac{1}{2}$), then as in the case of genetic inheritance and genetic relatedness, a child is far more related to its brothers and sisters than to its cousins. However, when children learn entirely from their mothers, they may be just as culturally related to their mother's sisters' children as to their own siblings. Similarly, when children learn mostly from their mothers, a man may be culturally more related to his sisters' children than he is to his own wife's children.

In general, if children are brought up mainly with their father's relatives, they are likely to perceive and respond to the ideas of their father's relatives. Conversely, the father in such a patrilocal family is more likely to pass wealth to his wife's children, who share most of his ideas, than to his sister's children who have learned many ideas from *their* father's relatives. Following this cultural logic through, a man in a natolocal society will find passing wealth to his sister's children, with whom he has lived and shared many ideas, more cognitively consistent than passing wealth to his wife's children.

The patrilocal residence pattern has a *matrilocal* counterpart, in which a married couple lives with the wife's mother (matrilocal) or more generally with the wife's kinship group (*uxorilocal*).[18] We use the less obscure term, matrilocal, to

Table 7.2. Cultural Coefficients of Relationship. Paternal Influence (P) Plus Maternal Influence (M) is Assumed to be 1.

Father and Child	Person and Sister's Child	Person and Brother's Child	Siblings	Cousins Related by 2 Sisters	Cousins Related by Brother and Sister	Cousins Related by 2 Brothers
P	$M^3 + MP^2$	$M^2P + P^3$	$M^2 + P^2$	$M^2P^2 + M^4$	$M^3P + MP^3$	$M^2P^2 + P^4$
0.0	1.000	0.000	1.000	1.000	0.000	0.000
0.2	0.544	0.136	0.680	0.435	0.109	0.027
0.4	0.312	0.208	0.520	0.187	0.125	0.082
0.6	0.208	0.312	0.520	0.082	0.125	0.187
0.8	0.136	0.544	0.680	0.027	0.109	0.435
1.0	0.000	1.000	1.000	0.000	0.000	1.000

cover uxorilocal as well. Fox saw the matrilocal household arising when sisters formed an economic team, perhaps as agriculturalists owning and tending a common plot of land, while the brothers pursued more mobile occupations.[19] This residence pattern leads to households or local groups containing several generations linked through females. The brothers, of course, leave their natal household upon marriage, but they maintain ties of various sorts with their sisters and their sisters' children as well as with their mother and her siblings. Matrilocal societies are less common than patrilocal societies but far more common than natolocal societies.

Like patrilocal residence, matrilocal residence is usually associated with institutionalization of marriage and coresidence of spouses. Fox pointed out that the matrilocal pattern can and often does work with a high turnover of spouses, whereas the patrilocal pattern does not.[20] Nevertheless, the fact of coresidence greatly increases the confidence of the husband that children born to his wife—while they are married and coresiding—are, in fact, his own children. The confidence of paternity should be roughly the same whether the husbands reside patrilocally or matrilocally. In either case, the man should be genetically more closely related to his wife's children than to his sisters' children. Thus, by genetic logic, both matrilocal and patrilocal residence should favor the custom whereby men pass wealth to their wives' children, since in doing so, men are most likely to benefit their own genes. However, cultural logic does not accord with genetic logic in the matrilocal situation.

Fox pointed out that the matrilocal residence almost inevitably gives rise to matrilineal ideology.[21] In our view, this causal relationship should exist, because matrilocal residence exposes children primarily to the influence of the mother and her relatives, meaning the children would grow up to be culturally more related to maternal kin than to paternal kin. Although a man residing with his wife's kin plays some role in the lives of his coresident children, his influence may be swamped by that of his wife and her relatives. If so, the man may share more ideas with his sisters' children than he shares with his own children (refer to table 7.2 where P is low). Closer cultural similarity to children of sisters should lead to matrilineal ideology and by consistency of ideas to matrilineal inheritance rules. In fact, most matrilocal societies have matrilineal inheritance, and virtually none have patrilineal inheritance as would be predicted from genetic logic.[22]

We should add that once established in a culture, inheritance rules may perpetuate themselves in a more fundamentally Darwinian sense. To illustrate, we consider the fate of the bearers of patrilineal inheritance ideas in an otherwise matrilineal society. Suppose a lone woman had the idea, inconsistent with the matrilineal ideology of her society, that husbands should pass wealth to their wives' children and not to their sisters' children. Even though she may not have persuaded her husband of this, assume that she was able to teach the idea to her own children, both male and female. Disregarding the marital or other strife created by the inconsistency, the idea is still almost certain to disappear. The woman's sons' children would inherit wealth accumulated by their fathers, but they would be unlikely to perpetuate their fathers' patrilineal inheritance ideas because they would be exposed to and likely learn the matrilineal inheritance ideas of their mothers and their mothers' relatives. The original woman's daughters' children would most likely learn patrilineal inheritance ideas, but they would not inherit wealth either from their mothers' brothers, who would have patrilineal ideas, or from their fathers, who would of course have matrilineal ideas, since they were raised in other families which had matrilineal ideas. As a result the descendants who did learn patrilineal inheritance ideas would not inherit any wealth and would thus be less likely to survive.

If we reversed the coin and looked at the fate of a novel matrilineal inheritance idea in a patrilineal society, the result would be similar—the idea would likely disappear by differential success of its bearers. The point is that inheritance ideas, once they are already very common in the society, are perpetuated *both* as part of an internally consistent kinship ideology *and* by the process of Darwinian subtraction of variant ideas.

⚜ ⚜

Although we are not writing a book on kinship, it is only fair that the reader should not be left with the impression that patriliny and matriliny are the only possible kinship ideologies. In some societies, a newly married couple may decide to live either with the wife's relatives or with the husband's relatives. This pattern is called *ambilocal* residence.[23] It leads to an *ambilineal* ideology, more commonly called *cognatic*, in which an individual has rights to membership in the kinship groups of both the father and the mother.[24] This ideology allows for flexibility in residence decisions based on the relative resources of the mother's group and the father's group.

The Yako of Nigeria have a double-descent system which superficially resembles the cognatic ideology, but which is actually quite different.[25] The Yako are urban people who reside patrilocally and inherit real estate patrilineally. Yet every member of a residence-based group is also a member of a scattered matrilineal group through which movable wealth is inherited matrilineally. Each individual belongs to two different groups with different functions and different means of recruiting new members. The Yako kinship groups are unilineal, meaning they recruit solely through one sex. In contrast, the cognatic individual belongs to two or more groups which have the same functions and which recruit new members through both sexes. Usually the individual's marital residence decision effectively cements ties to one group at the expense of ties to other groups in which he or she has membership rights. Nevertheless, the cognatic ideologies encourage the individual to affiliate equally with maternal and paternal relatives.

Finally, a married couple may establish their residence independent of either the husband's or the wife's relatives. This pattern is called *neolocal*.[26] It is the pattern most familiar to those of European extraction. Most Europeans have a cognatic ideology, in that they regard themselves as equally related to maternal and paternal relatives. However, they do not use this kinship ideology to form groups with any real permanence or function. As a result, this ideology has relatively little influence on the individual's behavior.

❧ ☙

We want to make clear the importance of distinguishing human behavior from human ideas about behavior. This distinction is crucial to understanding the evolution of human behavior. Our actual behavior may directly affect our Darwinian fitness, in terms of chances for survival and reproduction, but our ideas *cannot* do so *directly*. Ideas affect fitness only when they motivate behavior. As we mentally manipulate our ideas about the world and ourselves, fitness considerations only enter the process when we *perceive* a connection between fitness and behavior. The perception, once labeled, is itself an idea, which can evolve.

The appeal of Alexander's genetic explanation for the evolution of matriliny versus patriliny is its parsimony. Unfortunately for parsimonious explanations, the evolution of human cultural behavior is bound to the evolution of human ideas. Ideas are not directly subject to fitness differences as they are passed from person to person. The nagging problem is to specify how ideas are eliminated from human cultures and how this process relates to Darwinian fitness. In this chapter we have concentrated on the development and persistence of ideas. In the next chapter we will attempt to give a more complete picture of cultural change as we emphasize the elimination of maladaptive ideas.

CHAPTER EIGHT

THE LEGEND OF ESLOK

Once a man has committed himself at a series of choice points to particular courses of action, he may find himself in the end, even if he chose the better alternative at every point, in a position he would not have intended or preferred if he could have foreseen the whole consequence from the beginning. Nothing in the human condition leads to greater tragedies than this. —GEORGE CASPAR HOMANS[1]

The failure of the theory of natural selection by itself to account adequately for the retention and elimination of culturally transmitted ideas and behaviors has inevitably led to notions of cultural selection and to much debate over the adequacy of these notions. The ambiguity of such notions makes us reluctant to participate directly in this debate.[2] Nevertheless, we are confident that many of the ideas we have developed throughout this book can shed some light on the mechanisms of cultural change in human societies. Rather than bog down in the rich details of actual case histories, we have chosen to begin with a parable of cultural change which illustrates events that may have happened many times over in human history.

Consider the first meeting between Mephistopheles and the inhabitants of a small, isolated farming community called Koltinnopinnu.[3] Mephistopheles came to recruit souls for his Dark Kingdom and, of course, he had to devise a clever deceit to cover his real purpose. He came disguised as a

wandering holy man, pretending neither to speak nor understand the language of Koltinnopinnu, but nevertheless offering a strange assortment of gifts, or *kimto* as the Koltinnopinnuo called them. The farmers called the strange wanderer
Ev Kimtolinnin, which naturally enough meant "a man bearing gifts." The people were not overly suspicious of strangers;
however, they were wary of the strange gifts and at first
refused to accept them or even to touch them. Then Ev Tok
Killionnen, a farmer highly esteemed for his courage, stepped
forward to receive one of the *kimto*. Ev Tok's example persuaded a few of his friends also to take gifts, but most of the
farmers decided to wait and see what might happen next.
What happened was that the families of Ev Tok and the other
gift receivers were soon blessed by miraculous good fortune
of many kinds. Seeing this, more farmers came to the stranger
to receive *kimto* and within a few weeks, every grown man
in Koltinnopinnu had accepted a *kimt* from Ev Kimtolinnin.
His mission accomplished, Mephistopheles disappeared as
mysteriously as he had come.

The farmers of Koltinnopinnu had not even guessed that in
exchange for their good fortune, they had given up their
souls. And, of course, not one of them had any idea that
when he died his children would also soon die, because
children share the souls of their ancestors. Once every adult
in Koltinnopinnu had unwittingly made a bargain with
Mephistopheles, Koltinnopinnu was doomed to extinction.

It took a few years for the Koltinnopinnuo to figure out
what had really happened. As elder farmers died, whole
lineages died with them. In their anguished frustration, the
Koltinnopinnuo turned against Ev Tok Killionnen, because
he was the first to take a *kimt*. Ev Tok fled for his life and
wandered alone for years. He finally discovered Ikwalik,
a distant fertile valley wherein lived a farming society.[4] Ev Tok

settled among these Imkwalik farmers, learned their language and customs and was called Eslok, because the Imkwalik could not pronounce "Ev Tok." The Imkwalik were so impressed by Ev Tok's tale of Koltinnopinnu that it became part of their oral tradition and for generations thereafter was told by Imkwalik storytellers on special occasions. The mythical home of Eslok was called Kolinopuk.

Long after the death of Eslok, a shortage of farm land drove some venturesome families to set out from Ikwalik in search of the mythical valley of Kolinopuk. Eventually they found the valley, now uninhabited. They settled there and prospered. As the pioneers were all young, not one of them had been trained as a storyteller, so their children grew up without hearing the oral tradition told in the emotional, graphic way of the Imkwalik storytellers. Their parents who had come from Ikwalik could only vaguely remember the story of Eslok.

At about this time, Mephistopheles returned to the valley now called Kolinopuk. Once again, he was disguised as a wandering holy man bearing gifts. This time the settlers called him Mkwilkik, meaning "stranger" or, literally, "new man." The older people, who had heard the story of Eslok in Ikwalik, were very suspicious of Mkwilkik and his gifts. But many of the younger people dismissed the story as a fairytale and accused their parents of losing the venturous spirit which had led them to prosperity in Kolinopuk. A schism developed between those who heeded the fearful warning of Eslok and those who did not. Most of the older people and some of the younger adults who were susceptible to parental persuasion rejected the gifts and even threatened to kill Mkwilkik. The others, mostly young, accepted the gifts, reaped good fortune and gratefully protected the stranger until the day that he suddenly disappeared.

A month later, two brothers working together were accidently killed by a rock fall. One had rejected the gift of Mkwilkik; the other had accepted. The children of the second brother died mysteriously within a day of their father's death. One of the old men, who remembered the story of Eslok more clearly than the others, had predicted that those who accepted the gift would unknowingly kill their own children. The accident and subsequent deaths elevated this man to prominence as a prophet, and he was called Mkweslok ("man of Eslok"). Gradually over the following years, one family after another died out following the deaths of men who had accepted the gift of Mkwilkik. Fear, anger and helplessness drove the survivors to religious frenzy, inspired and led by Mkweslok. Mkweslok preached that Eslok had been a messenger of God and that Mkwilkik was the devil himself.

Centuries later the emotional impact of Mephistopheles' visit was firmly ingrained in the culture of Kolinopuk. The details of the visit and its awful consequences had become sacred knowledge, passed from the elders to young men in a fearful—even painful—and awe-inspiring initiation ritual. The children of Kolinopuk were taught to distrust strangers and everything else strange or new. Even the word for "new"—*ilkik*—had come to mean "evil" as well. Any person or object formally declared *ilkik* by the elders was immediately destroyed. The most tragic instance of this fear and mistrust occurred on the first visit to Kolinopuk in almost two hundred years by a man from the ancestral valley, Ikwalik.

Although the languages of the inhabitants of the two isolated valleys had drifted apart, there were still enough similarities to allow the visitor to communicate and to identify his home. Ikwalik had become almost a "paradise lost"—a place of goodness—in the religion of Kolinopuk. So the stranger was welcomed, at first.

In Ikwalik, the story of Eslok continued to be only one myth among many. The poor visitor had no inkling of the fanaticism in Kolinopuk. He started to tell of the tremendous advances in Ikwalik agriculture since the last contact with Kolinopuk. New varieties of grain had been developed, and new farming techniques and tools made the work easier and the harvests larger and more dependable. As the Imkwalik casually used a word sounding like *ilkik*, the audience of elder men grew noticeably uneasy. Then the Imkwalik visitor reached into his bag and drew out packets of the new grain seeds which he said he had brought as a gift to the people of Kolinopuk. Simultaneously, several men in the crowd pointed at the Imkwalik and shouted "Ilkik!" The man's body, the seeds and everything else he had brought were burned. The ashes were scattered in the wilderness beyond the valley.

Henceforth, Ikwalik was regarded as an enemy land and all captured Imkwalik visitors were publicly tortured before they were killed. Still the number of visitors increased as the inventive Imkwalik developed modes of transportation that reduced travel time between the valleys from several months to just under two weeks. The Imkwalik visitors also had sophisticated weapons that allowed some of them to escape and return to Ikwalik with news of the torture and killings. Soon the enraged Imkwalik people decided that the time had come to do something about their "barbarian" neighbors. An impressively equipped and well organized army was mounted and set against Kolinopuk. Even though the Mkolinopuk warriors still used the same kinds of primitive weapons as were brought to the valley by their pioneering forefathers, their fanatical ferocity greatly prolonged the war. Only gradually did the superior weaponry and organization of the invading Ikwalik army crush the more numerous and more courageous Mkolinopuk warriors. Toward the end, an esteemed Mkolinopuk warrior-leader suggested that instead of destroying the captured Ikwalik weapons, they should turn these weapons against the invaders. The elders declared the man *ilkik* and like all would-be innovators in Kolinopuk, he was executed immediately. The valley fell soon after.

The Imkwalik were open-hearted, open-minded people. They had no taste for further humiliating, much less destroying, the Mkolinopuk. As inventive in colonial administration as they were in weaponry, they attempted to draw the younger Mkolinopuk into the Ikwalik culture. The preconquest generations ignored the Ikwalik ways, as best they could, but the youngsters saw that power and success were associated with Ikwalik culture. Since the dreadful initiation rite had been banned, the youngsters did not share their elders' fierce distrust of strange ways. The story of Eslok was dismissed by Imkwalik teachers as nothing more than a myth invented by some ancient storytellers. Soon any idea or custom associated with Eslok was shunned as "primitive" and more and more people were converted to Ikwalik ways.

In the next century, the Imkwalik and their Mkolinopuk allies conquered the inhabitants of several more remote valleys. The valleys were linked by an ingenious system of rapid communication and transportation. Gradually, Ikwalik became Il Alik, a unified society and culture including the people of several valleys. Il Alik meant literally "New Land," and the word *alik* by itself came to mean both "new" and "holy."

The clever Mephistopheles had lain low during the peak of fanatical conservatism in Kolinopuk, but he kept an eye open for an opportunity to recruit more souls from that area. He, of course, recognized the emergence of Il Alik as his golden opportunity. Mephistopheles appeared in Kolinopuk in the same disguise, bearing the same strange assortment of miraculous gifts in seemingly limitless supply. The news of his arrival spread throughout Il Alik within a few days. Two weeks later the government of Il Alik officially declared the gifts *alik*. They also proclaimed Mephistopheles "Alikwan" and escorted him through all the valleys. Four weeks after his arrival, Mephistopheles had given a gift to every grown man of Il Alik.

The valleys of Il Alik were too far removed for news of disaster to reach the rest of the inhabited world. So centuries later, the Hettenite explorers had no idea that people once lived in those "newly discovered" valleys.

❧ ☙

Mephistopheles' gift resulted in immediate high rewards for those who accepted. Only later did the ancestors incur the inevitable high costs. It was the long *time lag* between an individual's perception of the rewards and his perception of the costs which led to disaster. Each man accepting the gift had committed himself irreversibly to a new behavior before perceiving the full consequences.

People can deal with the problem of time lags if they remember the full consequences of similar actions in the past. Myths, like the story of Eslok, can preserve historical events of the distant past and so serve as warnings or guidelines for the future. If events, like Mephistopheles's visits, occur very infrequently, knowledge of the events may become distorted. Myths may lose their emotional impact over the long intervals during which they seem unimportant. The accuracy and importance of cultural information can be better preserved if the information is made part of a sacred ritual. Rituals sanctify ideas, because rituals arouse strong emotions—fear, joy, anger and pain—and thus associate ideas directly with emotional experiences. Through ritual, abstract ideas have an emotional impact on people. As Roy A. Rappaport put it, "sanctification transforms the arbitrary into the necessary."[5] Ideas given emotional impact by rituals become sanctified ideas with which other ideas must be made consistent.

To illustrate the sanctification role of rituals, we had the Mkolinopuk convey the story of Eslok in a fear-arousing and painful initiation rite. Because of the strong emotional impact, boys coming of age were systematically made to fear and hate all *new* things, ideas and people. Consistent with their basic distrust of new things, the people of Kolinopuk killed the visitor from Ikwalik and destroyed the gifts he brought. Throughout our story, individuals made decisions consistent with their values and their perceptions of rewards and costs. For instance, Ev Tok valued his own self-image as a courageous man and this led him to accept the gift of Mephistopheles. High esteem (value) of Ev Tok by some others in the community led them to follow his example. All the people of Koltinnopinnu valued good fortune and this eventually led them to accept the gifts which had given good fortune to their neighbors. Finally, the very negative evaluation of death, especially the untimely deaths of friends and relatives, overwhelmed their own positive evaluations of the gifts. The Koltinnopinnuo rejected the gifts and everything associated with them, including Ev Tok, but too late.

We have distinguished two mechanisms for the elimination of ideas and customs. First, ideas can become cognitively inconsistent, because other referent ideas change. Second, ideas when translated into behavior can affect individual survival and even lead to differential extinction of entire cultural groups. Some, perhaps most, ideas and customs have little effect on individual fitness; that is, they have low *phenotypic* costs and rewards, as measured by their effects on individual survival and reproduction. William H. Durham has argued that human behaviors with high phenotypic costs and rewards evolve by natural selection acting on differences in Darwinian fitness.[6] We agree, with the following caution. The way natural selection, or what we prefer to call natural subtraction, acts on high-cost or high-reward behaviors depends on whether or not these costs and rewards are actually perceived as such by the people making behavioral decisions. If cultural values change in response to perceptions of true phenotypic costs and rewards, natural subtraction may be nipped in the bud.

Death is an obvious phenotypic cost which is clearly perceived as a cost by most people. The Koltinnopinnuo did not perceive the deadly effects of Mephistopheles' gifts until after their behavioral decisions were made. The whole society was eliminated by natural subtraction. However, in Kolinopuk, the deadly affects were perceived in time for many people to save themselves. Even though their culture changed radically in response to their perceptions, the historical continuity of this culture was not broken.

Cultures evolving in isolation from each other develop different ideas and different evaluations of the same ideas due to their different historical experiences. Human values are both the scars of the past and the portents of the future. When neighboring societies have different values, what the differences usually portend is conflict. Since cultural boundaries are necessarily boundaries to communication, even neighboring cultures tend to diverge. It is largely the accumulated differences in ideas and resulting behaviors that determine the outcome of conflict. Differential elimination of cultural groups has most likely been common in the evolutionary history of our species.

Since human groups always have some genetic differences, sociobiologists have argued that group selection may have been responsible for the genetic evolution of human social behavior.[7] Cultural group subtraction does not necessarily imply genetic group selection. Though ancestral ideas and customs usually accompany conquered warriors to their graves, the warriors' genes may survive in their descendants who adopt new ways. Indeed, conquests are normally followed by gene exchange which prevents further genetic drift between groups. Furthermore, the Darwinian fitness of "defeated" genotypes may actually increase after conquest as conquered people adopt the customs of their conquerors and prosper.

A critical characteristic of any cultural group is its receptivity to new ideas. Historical experiences may push a culture to become relatively open or closed to new ideas. However, cultures that become too closed often suffer the fate of Kolinopuk, while those that become too open may go the way of Il Alik. An intermediate position, probably achieved through a diversity of individual attitudes toward innovation, is no doubt the healthiest from an evolutionary point of view. Probably societies are more likely to become too closed than to become too open. The operation of cognitive consistency creates a bias toward conservatism, simply because new ideas must generally fit in with those already well established.

⚜ ⚜

If the rise of Il Alik seems like an allegory of the relatively recent rise of "European" cultural dominance throughout the world, it is because we designed it so. The competitive success of European cultures has depended greatly on the high value attached to innovation and change. Innovations are accepted mainly for their short-term rewards, with little thought given to long-term consequences. Successful innovators are greatly rewarded. In their haste, European cultures have created an unprecedented world which demands yet more rapid change. Only continued innovation can keep this new world from collapsing.

The lesson of Koltinnopinnu and Il Alik is that rapid change may render useless a society's ability to eliminate or avoid cultural mistakes. The only thing that stopped the further spread of the gift of Mephistopheles was lack of communication with the larger world. In Il Alik, the spread of the cultural mistake was speeded by the rapid communication and transportation between valleys all sharing the same culture, including the exceptionally positive evaluation of new ideas.

Communication between different cultures can, of course, be very beneficial. Different societies generate a diversity of cultural experiments. If they are communicating sufficiently to compare the results of their various experiments, the societies can learn from each other's successes and mistakes. Remember that Ev Tok carried the story of disaster in Koltinnopinnu to Ikwalik, and this story eventually saved Kolinopuk from total elimination. More generally, we can say that communication and comparison by *different* cultures can both speed acceptance of beneficial traits and deter the spread of harmful ones.

Unfortunately, rapid and frequent communication between cultures has a homogenizing effect which reduces cultural diversity. The spreading of European cultures through conquest and, more recently, by rapid transportation and communication, has lowered the boundaries to worldwide spread of innovations. Much of the modern world may already be facing the difficulties of a monoculture. The loss of diversity not only means loss of cultural material with which people can start out on new paths of cultural evolution; it also means that unforeseen foul-ups can sweep through the whole world. There is nothing left for our fast-changing, increasingly homogeneous world but to rely on our human abilities to anticipate the consequences of our actions. People must choose innovations as wisely as they can and hope for good luck.

We have no policy recommendations. It is impossible to return willingly to a world of small, isolated, slowly changing cultural units. In many respects, the beneficiaries of European cultures have never had it so good, and the greatest desire of the have-nots is to get their share. In describing the evolutionary risks of modern progress, we only make the point, as have so many others, that people should not be surprised if the whole house of cards comes tumbling down. On the other hand, neither should we be surprised if by some combination of chance and wisdom the delicate structure stays upright. Nothing in evolutionary history is more impressive than the resilience and resourcefulness of human beings. The future will probably not be as bright as we hope, but equally likely, it will not be as dismal as we fear.

NOTES

Preface

1. Edward O. Wilson, *Sociobiology: The New Synthesis* (Cambridge, Mass.: Belknap Press of Harvard University Press, 1975), and, more recently, Edward O. Wilson, *On Human Nature* (Cambridge, Mass.: Harvard University Press, 1978). For a recent review of the controversy in the popular press, see Tom Bethell, "Burning Darwin to Save Marx," *Harper's*, December 1978.

1. The Gene's Agent

1. Claude Lévi-Strauss, *Tristes Tropiques*. John and Doreen Weightman, trans. (New York: Atheneum, 1974).

2. See Marvin Harris, *The Rise of Anthropological Theory: A History of Theories of Culture* (New York: Crowell, 1968). Also, for an excellent recent review of Darwinian ideas applied to cultural evolution, see William H. Durham, "The Adaptive Significance of Cultural Behavior," *Human Ecology* (1976), 4:89–121, and the several discussions of Durham's article which appeared in *Human Ecology* (1977), 5:49–68.

3. We are referring to the structural anthropology of Claude Lévi-Strauss and his followers. For a recent review, see Bob Scholte, "The Structural Anthropology of Claude Lévi-Strauss," in J. J. Honigmann, ed., *Handbook of Social and Cultural Anthropology* (Chicago: Rand McNally, 1973), pp. 637–716.

4. Jacques Monod, *Chance and Necessity: An Essay on the Natural Philosophy of Modern Biology*. Austryn Wainhouse, trans. (New York: Knopf, 1971), p. 20.

5. Richard Dawkins, *The Selfish Gene* (Oxford: Oxford University Press, 1976).

6. Our thanks and apologies to stockbrokers Robert A. Schneider

and James Jay Fritton for information used in this analogy of genes and investors.

7. For more detailed comparisons of theories in the biological and social sciences, see Luigi Cavalli-Sforza, "Similarities and Dissimilarities of Socio-Cultural and Biological Evolution," in F. R. Hodson, D. G. Kendall, and P. Tantu, eds., *Mathematics in the Archaeological and Historical Sciences* (Edinburgh: Edinburgh University Press, 1971), pp. 535–41, and Peter J. Richerson, "Ecology and Human Ecology: A Comparison of Theories in the Biological and Social Sciences," *American Ethnologist* (1977), 4:1–26.

2. The Cybernetic Lizard vs. The Toxic Ants

1. Edward O. Wilson, *On Human Nature*, p. 65.

2. Our use of the term *program* is very similar to the use of the term *strategy* in the psychological literature. For example, see K. H. Brookshire, "Vertebrate Learning: Evolutionary Divergences," in R. B. Masterton, M. E. Bitterman, C. B. G. Campbell and N. Hotton, eds., *Evolution of Brain and Behavior in Vertebrates* (Hillsdale, N.J.: Lawrence Erlbaum Associates, 1976), pp. 191–216.

3. For references to bait-shyness in rats see S. H. Revusky, "Aversion to Sucrose Produced by Contingent X-Irradiation: Temporal and Dosage Parameters," *Journal of Comparative and Physiological Psychology* (1968), 65:17–22; and J. C. Smith and D. L. Roll, "Trace Conditioning with X-Rays as the Aversive Stimulus," *Psychonomic Science* (1967), 9:11–12.

4. A modern discussion of the question of animal consciousness and emotions has been written by Donald R. Griffin, *The Question of Animal Awareness: Evolutionary Continuity of Mental Experience* (New York: Rockefeller University Press, 1976). See also Richard L. Gregory, "Consciousness," in Ronald Duncan and Miranda Weston-Smith, eds., *The Encyclopaedia of Ignorance* (New York: Pergamon Press, 1977), pp. 273–81.

5. The *genome* is defined by geneticists as the complete genetic constitution of an individual.

6. For a survey of the field, see Richard Atkinson, Gordon Bower and Edward Carothers, *An Introduction to Mathematical Learning Theory* (New York: Wiley, 1965).

7. Robert Bush and Frederick Mosteller, *Stochastic Models for Learning* (New York: Wiley, 1955).

8. High and low values of α correspond to differences in what psychologists call "probability learning." A low value of α leads to reward following and a high value leads to nonrandom probability matching.

9. For a more complete discussion of the evolution of learning in patchy environments, see Stevan J. Arnold, "The Evolution of a Special Class of Modifiable Behaviors in Relation to Environmental Pattern," *American Naturalist* (1978), 112:415–27; and H. Ronald Pulliam, "Learning to Forage Optimally," in Al Kamil, ed., *Foraging Behavior* (New York: Garland Press, 1980).

10. Peter H. Klopfer, personal communication to Pulliam.

3. Emotion and Decision

1. David P. Barash, *Sociobiology and Behavior* (New York: Elsevier, 1977), p. 311.

2. François Jacob, "Evolution and Tinkering," *Science* (1977), 196:1161–66.

3. George Edgin Pugh, *The Biological Origin of Human Values* (New York: Basic Books, 1977).

4. Pugh, p. 67.

5. Pugh, p. 67.

6. Pugh, p. 66.

7. Pugh, p. 30.

8. Charles Darwin, *The Expression of Emotions in Man and Animals* (D. Appleton & Co., 1896). See also Howard E. Gruber, *Darwin on Man: A Psychological Study of Scientific Creativity* (New York: Dutton, 1974).

9. Darwin, *Expression of Emotions*, p. 138.

10. Darwin, pp. 142–43.

11. Virginia Woolf was quoted by Ronald Melzack in "The Perception of Pain," in Neil Chalmer, Roberta Crawley and Steven P. R. Rose, eds., *The Biological Bases of Behaviour* (London: Harper and Row, 1971), p. 179.

12. Patrick Wall, "Why Do We Not Understand Pain?" in Ronald

Duncan and Miranda Weston-Smith, eds., *The Encyclopaedia of Ignorance* (New York: Pergamon Press, 1977), p. 362.

13. Wall, p. 364.

14. The reference to societies where the pain of childbirth is felt by the husband comes from Melzack, "The Perception of Pain," p. 190.

15. Wall, "Why Do We Not Understand Pain?" p. 364.

16. James Olds, *Reticular Formation of the Brain* (Boston: Little, Brown, 1958), p. 173. See also James Olds, "Pleasure Centers in the Brain," *Scientific American* (1956), 195:106–16.

17. C. M. Davis, "Self-Selection of Diets by Newly Weaned Infants," *American Journal of Diseases of Children* (1928), 36:651–79, and C. M. Davis, "Results of the Self-Selection of Diets by Young Children," *Canadian Medical Association Journal* (1939), 41:257.

18. M. Nachman and L. P. Cole, "Role of Taste in Specific Hungers," *Handbook of Sensory Physiology* (1971), 4:337–62.

19. Nachman and Cole, p. 340.

20. Nachman and Cole, p. 340.

21. John Bowlby, *Attachment and Loss*, vol. 2: *Separation* (New York: Basic Books, 1973).

22. Bowlby, p. 96.

23. Bowlby, p. 104.

24. Bowlby, p. 102.

25. Harry F. Harlow and Robert R. Zimmerman, "Affectional Responses in the Infant Monkey," *Science* (1959), 130:421–32, and Harry F. Harlow, "Development of Affection in Primates," in E. L. Bliss, ed., *Roots of Behavior* (New York: Harper & Row, 1962), pp. 157–66.

26. Niko Tinbergen, *The Study of Instinct* (Oxford: Oxford University Press, 1951).

27. See, for example, R. Legrand, "Successful Aggression as the Reinforcer for Runway Behavior of Mice," *Psychonomic Science* (1970), 20:303–5.

28. John Archer, "The Organization of Aggression and Fear in Vertebrates," in P. P. G. Bateson and Peter Klopfer, eds., *Perspectives In Ethology* (New York: Plenum Press, 1976), pp. 231–98.

29. E. O. Wilson estimated that "the selection pressures of the hunter-gatherer existence have persisted for over 99 percent of human genetic evolution," in *On Human Nature* (Cambridge, Mass.: Harvard University Press, 1978), p. 84.

4. Shortcuts To Learning

1. Konrad Lorenz, "Der Kumpan in der Umwelt des Vogels," *Journal für Ornithologie* (1935), 83:137–213, 289–413. For an excellent recent review of imprinting, see Klaus Immelmann, "Ecological Significance of Imprinting and Early Learning," *Annual Review of Ecology and Systematics* (1975), 6:15–37.

2. For a more detailed consideration of habitat imprinting by birds, see Peter Klopfer, "Behavioral Aspects of Habitat Selection: The Role of Early Experience," *Wilson Bulletin* (1963), 75:15–22, and Peter Klopfer and J. P. Hailman, "Habitat Selection in Birds," *Advances in the Study of Behavior* (1965), 1:279–303.

3. For a general account of ethology which discusses the terms "releaser" and "fixed action patterns" in detail, see Irenäus Eibl–Eibesfeldt, *Ethology: The Biology of Behavior* (New York: Holt, Rinehart & Winston, 1970).

4. Konrad Lorenz, *Studies in Animal and Human Behavior*, vol. 1, (Cambridge, Mass.: Harvard University Press, 1970), p. 246.

5. There is a current debate among neurophysiologists as to the exact nature of learning and memory. For a recent point of view, see Henry A. Buchtel and Giovanni Berlucchi, "Learning and Memory and the Nervous System," in Ronald Duncan and Miranda Weston-Smith, eds., *The Encyclopaedia of Ignorance* (New York: Pergamon Press, 1977), pp. 283–97. A more general discussion has been written by E. Roy John in *Mechanisms of Memory* (New York: Academic Press, 1967).

6. P. P. G. Bateson, S. P. R. Rose, and G. Horn, "Imprinting: Lasting Effects of Uracil Incorporation into Chick Brain," *Science* (1973), 181:576–78. See also P. P. G. Bateson, "The Nature of Early Learning," *Science* (1974), 183: 740–41.

7. Peter Marler, "On Strategies of Behavioral Development," in G. Baerends, C. Beer and A. Manning, eds., *Function and Evolution in Behaviour* (Oxford: Clarendon Press, 1975), pp. 224–27, and Peter Marler and Miwako Tamura, "Culturally Transmitted Patterns of Vocal Behavior in Sparrows," *Science* (1964), 146:1483–86. An excellent review of learned bird songs is Fernando Nottebohm's "The Origins of Vocal Learning," *American Naturalist* (1972), 106:116–40.

8. For a fascinating account of the cultural transmission of song dialects, see Luis F. Baptista's "Song Dialects and Demes in Seden-

tary Populations of the White-Crowned Sparrow (*Zonotrichia leu-cophrys nuttali*)," *University of California Publications in Zoology* (1975), 105:1–52.

9. See also Joan G. Stevenson, "Song as a Reinforcer," in William Van de Kloot, Charles Walcott and Benjamin Dane, eds., *Readings in Behavior* (New York: Holt, Rinehart & Winston, 1974), pp. 499–512.

10. Bateson reported these recent studies to Pulliam in a personal communication.

11. Paul J. Greenwood, Paul H. Harvey and Christopher M. Perrins, "Inbreeding and Dispersal in the Great Tit," *Nature* (1978), 271:52–54.

12. For a recent review of observational learning, see B. G. Galef, Jr., "Social Transmission of Acquired Behavior: A Discussion of Traditional Social Learning in Vertebrates," *Advances in the Study of Behavior* (1976), 6:77–100.

13. In particular, see E. R. P. John, P. Chesler, F. Bartlett and I. Victor, "Observational Learning in Cats," *Science* (1968), 159: 1489–91, and P. Chesler, "Maternal Influence in Learning by Observation in Kittens," *Science* (1969), 166: 901–3.

14. P. Jouventin, G. Pasteur and J. P. Cambéfort, "Observational Learning of Baboons and Avoidance of Mimics: Exploratory Tests," *Evolution* (1977), 31:214–18.

15. For reviews of the Japanese macaque work, see Denzaburo Miyadi, "Social Life of Japanese Monkeys," *Science* (1964), 143: 783–86, and J. Itani and A. Nishimura, "The Study of Infrahuman Culture in Japan," *Symposium of the Fourth International Congress of Primatology*, vol. 1 (Basel: Karger, 1973), pp. 26–50.

16. J. Itani, "On the Acquisition and Propagation of a New Food Habit," *Primates* (1958), 1:84–98, and D. Miyadi, "On Some New Habits and Their Propagation in Japanese Monkey Groups," *Proceedings, XV International Congress of Zoology* (1959), 857–60.

5. Social Exchange And Cognitive Balance

1. George Caspar Homans, *Social Behavior: Its Elementary Forms*, rev. ed. (New York: Harcourt, Brace, Jovanovich, 1974).

2. Homans, p. 27.

3. Darwin, *The Expression of Emotions in Man and Animals* (D. Appleton, 1896). p. 364.

4. Jack W. Thibaut and Harold H. Kelley, *The Social Psychology of Groups* (New York: Wiley, 1959).

5. Homans, *Social Behavior*, p. 37.

6. The fascinating details of attribution and probability estimation, as cognitive processes, are best left for the reader to pursue with Harold H. Kelley, "The Process of Causal Attribution," *American Psychologist* (1973), 28:107–28, and A. Tversky and D. Kahneman, "Judgment under Uncertainty: Heuristics and Biases," *Science* (1974), 185:1124–31.

7. R. P. Abelson, E. Aronson, W. J. McGuire, T. M. Newcomb, M. J. Rosenberg, and P. H. Tannenbaum, eds., *Theories of Cognitive Consistency: A Sourcebook* (Chicago: Rand McNally, 1968).

8. Fritz Heider, *The Psychology of Interpersonal Relations* (New York: Wiley, 1958). A similar formulation was developed by D. Cartwright and F. Harary, who introduced the linear graph treatment of consistency problems in "Structural Balance: A Generalization of Heider's Theory," *Psychological Review* (1956), 63:277–93.

9. James A. Davis, "Structural Balance, Mechanical Solidarity, and Interpersonal Relations," *American Journal of Sociology* (1963), 68:444–62. We recommend this paper as probably the most straightforward available presentation of the subject of cognitive balance and its application to social behavior.

10. Davis, p. 446.

11. This figure is Davis's figure 1, redrawn by permission of the publisher.

12. From William Shakespeare's *Romeo and Juliet*.

13. We recommend Everett M. Rogers and F. F. Shoemaker, *Communication of Innovations: A Cross-Cultural Approach* (New York: Free Press, 1971) as the best survey of the field.

14. Bryce Ryan and N. C. Gross, "The Diffusion of Hybrid Seed Corn in Two Iowa Communities," *Rural Sociology* (1943), 8:15–24.

15. Our figure 5.3 is figure 3.3 in R. L. Hamblin, R. B. Jacobsen and J. L. L. Miller, *A Mathematical Theory of Social Change* (New York: Wiley, 1973), redrawn by permission of the publisher. The data were taken by these authors from Ryan and Gross, cited above.

16. Alex O. Thio, "A Reconsideration of the Concept of Adopter-

Innovation Compatibility in Diffusion Research," *Sociological Quarterly* (1971), 12:56–68.

17. Davis, "Structural Balance."

18. Constantine A. Yeracaris, "Political Conflict and the Diffusion of Innovations," *Rural Sociology* (1970), 35:488–99.

6. The Mathematics Of Culture

1. Jacques Monod, *Chance and Necessity*, p. 154.

2. For a modern introduction to the mathematical theory of genetic evolution, we recommend James F. Crow and Motoo Kimura, *An Introduction to Population Genetics Theory* (New York: Harper & Row, 1970), and Richard Lewontin, *The Genetic Basis of Evolutionary Change* (New York: Columbia University Press, 1974).

3. Luigi Cavalli-Sforza and Marcus Feldman, "Models for Cultural Inheritance I. Group Mean and Within Group Variation," *Theoretical Population Biology* (1973), 4:42–55; Luigi Cavalli-Sforza and Marcus Feldman, "Cultural versus Biological Inheritance: Phenotypic Transmission from Parents to Children (A Theory of the Effect of Parental Phenotypes on Children's Phenotypes)," *Human Genetics* (1973), 25:618–37; Luigi Cavalli-Sforza, "The Role of Plasticity in Biological and Cultural Evolution," *Annals of the New York Academy of Science* (1974), 231:43–59; Marcus Feldman and Luigi Cavalli-Sforza, "Models for Cultural Inheritance II. A General Linear Model," *Annals of Human Biology* (1975), 2:215–26; Luigi Cavalli-Sforza, "Cultural and Biological Evolution: A Theoretical Inquiry," *Ateneo Parmense* (1975), 11:19–31; Marcus Feldman and Luigi Cavalli-Sforza, "Cultural and Biological Evolutionary Processes. Selection for a Trait Under Complex Transmission," *Theoretical Population Biology* (1976), 9:238–59. See also Peter J. Richerson and Robert Boyd, "A Dual Inheritance Model of the Human Evolutionary Process I. Basic Postulates and a Simple Model," *Journal of Social Biology Structure* (1978), 1:127–54.

4. The quote is from Luigi Cavalli-Sforza, "The Theory of Biological Evolution, Its Relation with Statistics and Its Extension to Cultural Evolution," *Rendic. Accademia Nazionale dei Lincei. Centro Linceo* (1977), 37, p. 70.

5. Cavalli-Sforza and Feldman, "Models for Cultural Inheritance I," p. 45.

6. Cavalli-Sforza and Feldman, "Cultural versus Biological Inheritance," p. 619.

7. Feldman and Cavalli-Sforza, "Models for Cultural Inheritance II," p. 216.

8. Cavalli-Sforza and Feldman, "Models for Cultural Inheritance I," p. 45.

9. This equation also differs by a factor $(1 - g)^2$ from that given by Cavalli-Sforza and Feldman, "Models for Cultural Inheritance I," p. 46.

10. Cavalli-Sforza and Feldman, "Models for Culture Inheritance I," p. 46. The equation given by Cavalli-Sforza and Feldman differs by a factor $(1 - g)^2$ from our equation 6.7. This is because in their original model they multiplied the random error by $(1 - g)$.

11. Cavalli-Sforza and Feldman, "Models for Cultural Inheritance I," p. 46.

12. *Cultural selection*, like genetic selection, acts on variation in Darwinian fitness, but for cultural selection, unlike genetic selection, the mechanism of inheritance is social learning. Cultural selection is only one mechanism by which cultural traits evolve. *Cultural retention* is a more general term which includes cultural selection *and* the differential retention of learned behaviors due to differences in cognitive consistency. For further discussion of cultural retention, see Eugene E. Ruyle, "Genetic and Cultural Pools: Some Suggestions for a Unified Theory of Biocultural Evolution," *Human Ecology* (1973), 1:201–15, and William H. Durham, "The Adaptive Significance of Cultural Behavior," *Human Ecology* (1976), 4:89–121.

13. See Feldman and Cavalli-Sforza, "Models for Cultural Inheritance II," pp. 219–221.

14. The diffusion of the new drug is discussed in James S. Coleman, *Introduction to Mathematical Sociology* (London: Collier MacMillan, 1964). The original reference is to James S. Coleman, Elihu Katz, and Herbert Menzel, "The Diffusion of an Innovation among Physicians," *Sociometry* (1957), 20:253–70.

15. For other examples of the application of mathematical models to sociology, see R. L. Hamblin, R. B. Jacobsen, and J. L. L. Miller, *A Mathematical Theory of Social Change* (New York: Wiley, 1973).

Our figure 6.10 is figure 4.4 in *A Mathematical Theory*, redrawn by permission of the publisher.

7. The Evolution of Ideas

1. Marshall Sahlins, *The Use and Abuse of Biology* (Ann Arbor: University of Michigan Press, 1976), p. 17.

2. Our concept that ideas may be accepted or rejected on the basis of cognitive consistency should be compared to that proposed by Eugene E. Ruyle, in "Genetic and Cultural Pools," that cultural traits are accepted or rejected on the basis of "satisfaction." We agree with Durham's criticism, in "Adaptive Significance of Cultural Behavior," that the satisfaction criterion is circular. Cognitive consistency, on the other hand, is defined by operations independent of acceptance or rejection.

3. Robin Fox, *Kinship and Marriage: An Anthropological Perspective* (Baltimore: Penguin Books, 1967). See especially pp. 41–50 and 77–83.

4. Fox, p. 85.

5. Fox, pp. 100–101.

6. Fox, pp. 101–102.

7. Fox, p. 101.

8. This study of incest is summarized by Edward O. Wilson in *On Human Nature* (Cambridge, Mass.: Harvard University Press, 1978), p. 37.

9. Fox, *Kinship and Marriage*, p. 84.

10. Fox, p. 84.

11. William D. Hamilton, "The Genetical Theory of Social Behaviour," I and II, *Journal of Theoretical Biology* (1964), 7:1-52.

12. The note about J. B. S. Haldane came from John Maynard Smith, personal communication.

13. For examples, see Pierre van den Berghe and David P. Barash, "Inclusive Fitness and Human Family Structure," *American Anthropologist* (1977), 79:897–23, and Penelope J. Greene, "Promiscuity, Paternity, and Culture," *American Ethnologist* (1978), 5:151–59.

14. Richard D. Alexander, "Natural Selection and the Analysis of Human Sociality," in C. E. Goulden, ed., *The Changing Scenes in Natural Sciences, 1776-1976* (Philadelphia: Philadelphia Academy of Natural Sciences, 1977), pp. 283-337.

15. Alexander, "Natural Selection."

16. For a similar argument, see Richerson and Boyd, "A Dual Inheritance Model of the Human Evolutionary Process," *Journal of Social Biology Structure* (1978), pp. 146–51.

17. We are assuming the different children in the same family have independent learning probabilities; that is, what one child has learned does not *per se* affect what another child learns.

18. Fox, *Kinship and Marriage*, p. 84.

19. Fox, pp. 81–82.

20. Fox, p. 82.

21. Fox, p. 121.

22. See, for example, Richerson and Boyd, "Dual Inheritance Model," p. 148.

23. Fox, *Kinship and Marriage*, p. 85.

24. Fox, p. 47.

25. Fox, pp. 135–138.

26. Fox, p. 85.

8. The Legend of Eslok

1. Homans, *Social Behavior*, p. 33.

2. See Eugene E. Ruyle, F. T. Cloak, Jr., L. B. Slobodkin and William H. Durham, "The Adaptive Significance of Cultural Behavior: Comments and Reply," *Human Ecology* (1977), 5:49–67.

3. *Koltinnopinnu* rhymes with "EVERYTHING you DO." It is the name of an imaginary place and also the name of a person from that place. Two or more such people are called *Koltinnopinnuo*, the suffix -*o* meaning "plural." Similarly, the plural of *kimt* ("gift") is *kimto*. Other Koltinnopinnu words appearing in this story are *ev* ("person" or "man"), *tok* ("brave" or "fearless"), *Killionnen* (a family name of unknown meaning), *kimtolinnin* ("bearing gifts"). All letters are pronounced as in the phonetic alphabet (similar to Spanish). The accent or emphasis is always on the first syllable.

4. *Ikwalik* is the name of an imaginary place, and *Imkwalik* is a person or persons who come from that place. *Ikwalik* sounds like "equality." The name can be broken down to a prefix *i-* ("land," "place" or "country"), an infix -*kw*- ("from" or "of") and a base word -*alik* ("good," but this word later came to mean both "new" and "holy"). The infix (or prefix) -*m*- means "person." The compound

prefix *Imkw-* means "person(s) of the land of." Similarly, *Kolinopuk* (pronounced KOLinopuk) is a place and *Mkolinopuk* is a person from that place. This second place name arose from *Imkwalik* attempts to pronounce *Koltinnopinnu*. In the same way, *Eslok* arose from *Ev Tok*. Eslok is pronounced "ES-lok" (the *Imkwalik* mispronounced *Ev Tok* because their language has no *t* or *v* sounds). As in the *Koltinnopinnu* language, *Ikwalik* and *Kolinopuk* letters are pronounced phonetically.

    5. Roy A. Rappaport, "The Sacred in Human Evolution," *Annual Review of Ecology and Systematics* (1971), 2:23–44, p. 35.

    6. Durham, "Adaptive Significance of Cultural Behavior," pp. 101–6.

    7. See, in particular, E. O. Wilson, *Sociobiology*, pp. 106–29 and pp. 547–75.

INDEX